SACRED BOND

Black Men and Their Mothers

By Keith Michael Brown

Foreword by James McBride

Photographs by Adger W. Cowans

LITTLE, BROWN AND COMPANY
Boston, New York, Toronto, London

First Edition

Library of Congress Cataloging-in-Publication Data

Sacred bond : Black men and their mothers / [compiled] by Keith Michael Brown;
photographs by Adger W. Cowans. — 1st ed.
         p.   cm.
ISBN 0-316-10556-2
1. Afro-American men — Family relationships — Anecdotes.
2. Mothers and sons — United States — Anecdotes.
I. Brown, Keith Michael.
E185.86.S23 1998
306.874'3 — dc21   98-20757

10 9 8 7 6 5 4 3 2 1

Q-HAW

Book Design by Madeleine Corson Design, San Francisco

Published simultaneously in Canada by Little, Brown & Company (Canada) Limited

Printed in the United States of America

To my mother, Constance Brown,
my father, Joseph R. Brown,
and his mother, Vivian Ruffin Brown;
also to my brother Richard Scott
and in loving memory of my brother Marc Joseph

Adger W. Cowans dedicates
the photographs to his
mother, Beatrice L. Cowans,
and his father, Adger W. Cowans

CONTENTS

The women you are about to meet you've seen every day of your life. You've seen them on the subway, their stockings ripped, pants too short, exhausted, snoring over a newspaper on the way home from work. You've seen them on the side of the highway, standing next to a broken-down sedan with bald tires, smoke hissing out its hood. You've seen them running through office buildings, dressed to the nines, huffing and puffing as they head out to a suburban football field to sit on cold bleachers to watch some kid kick a six-yard punt. They are rich, poor, black, white, Latino, Asian, and "other." Many are middle class. Some are not. All are heroes and champions, and this book is about the dreams they made possible.

These are women committed to the honor of motherhood, and the young men whom Keith Brown has carefully gathered speak about them in ways that only a son can speak, with a love that only a son can feel. For that reason, the stories you are about to experience will hit you square in the chest. Some will make you laugh out loud. Others will bring tears to your eyes. None will leave you unmoved. In a way, these stories humanize a part of America that too many of us see from behind the wheel of a locked car. Yet behind the shuttered windows of that "other" America — the neat, tiny homes of Compton in LA, the tired, sagging rowhouses of Baltimore, the iron-barred housing projects in Brooklyn, the tall high-rises in Seattle, and even the more gracious, stately homes of Chicago — real work is going on: Dreams are being nurtured, champions are being created, artists are being formed, scientists are being anointed, boys are becoming men.

There is a special relationship between a mother and son that defies race and class. The bonding, however healthy or unhealthy it may be, usually lasts a lifetime. For the women in this book — women of various races and colors — this bond carried even deeper meaning, because each of them lived with the knowledge that the son they were raising would one day be viewed with great hostility by society. There's nothing worse than knowing that the seventeen-year-old you just kissed goodbye that morning, the one whom you spent your life nurturing, the one whom you taught to say "thank you" and "you're welcome," the one who climbed into your bed each night with his Superman comics, might find himself on the wrong end of a cop's smoking gun that afternoon because he bears the same skin color as some seventeen-year-old who committed the latest atrocity on last night's Action News. There's no feeling like that fear; that deep, deep, hope-to-God-it-don't-happen-to-mine fear. It takes a special kind of woman to look beyond that, to rise above that, to place her hope in a knowing God and a trusting society in order to raise a boy without bitterness, without fear, without anger, to raise a boy who respects a society that has so little respect for him. The men who speak on the ensuing pages prove that these women were up to the task. They defy every stereotype of what a minority man is supposed to be. They are not the hooligans you see chest-thumping in the NBA, or angry, bitter gangsta rappers playing into stereotypes, or lousy comedians cracking foul-mouthed jokes on BET. They are admiring, gentle, insightful, brilliant, strong men. Men you could ride the subway with. Men you could march with. Men you could love. That's because they, as children, were loved.

For years our society swallowed the mythical Donna Reed image of motherhood. She was diffident, feminine, beautiful, never angry, upper middle class, married, and, of course, white. In reality no such creature exists. All good mothers struggle. All good mothers suffer for their children. All good mothers show dignity, courage, bravery, anger, patience, pride, and humility. Here are a few of their stories. It is my deepest hope that you have had the honor of knowing someone of like royalty.

— JAMES McBRIDE, AUTHOR OF *THE COLOR OF WATER*

TILL DEATH DO US PART

——

I thought my mother was too fragile to withstand the pain of my brother's death. He was her firstborn son. We had celebrated his thirtieth birthday just months before, and I believed his death would drive my mother into a depression so deep that it would immobilize her. But I was wrong. I watched my mother — a woman who used to cry when we teased her — stand before 450 people at my brother's funeral and read a letter she had written to him two days after he had passed away.

To my dearest son Marc,

I know you are gone in body, but I know your spirit and love are in this room and can hear these words. Many things have happened in the past seven weeks that will never be forgotten, nor should they be. I still find it very difficult to put into words my innermost feelings about you and the traumatic yet very spiritual experience we all went through this spring. It is an experience that will remain with me all the days of my life.

We had no idea you were HIV positive until you came home and entered the hospital. I remember you looked up at me and said, "I have AIDS." You started to say "Why me?" But then you stopped and said, "No, why not me." You also started to say you were sorry. But I stopped you.

You have done nothing in your life but make me and your father proud. You are our first son and have given me enough joy to last until I join you once again. Yes, you were gay. It was difficult to accept at first but I learned to accept you for everything that you are. All of our children are different and we have to learn to accept those differences. It is the only way.

We discussed so many things in that little hospital room and we learned so much about one another. Letting you go was the most painful experience of my life. But you gave your father and me the faith to let you go and let God take over. You left us with great strength to survive.

Six and one half weeks, that's all it took. It seemed forever. I wish I could have changed places with you — anything but this. How can I possibly handle the days and nights ahead? The pain and suffering are gone for you now. I know you are in a place where there is no such thing.

Marc, I thank God you trusted us enough to come home. I thank God every day that you didn't die alone, that I could be with you. I will never ever understand how families can turn their backs on their children and loved ones afflicted with this horrible disease.

Maybe parents when they have children should take vows similar to the ones they take when they marry, "to love and to cherish, for richer or poorer, in sickness and in health, till death do us part."

I love you,

Mom

As these words streamed from her heart, her bottom lip quivered slightly. I cried. At that moment, I saw my mother's strength and I understood the depth of her love for us, her three sons. And I painfully understood the depth of my mother's suffering — one-third of everything she and my father had worked and lived for was taken from them. My mother, the first woman in our blue-collar community to send her sons off to college and to watch each one of them graduate, had now become another "first": the first to lose a child to the AIDS virus. But she never bowed in defeat.

My brothers and I were raised by a woman who wore the same winter coat for ten years, and only once went away on vacation, so we could have the things we needed. She never resented it and only rarely complained. She spent as much time at our schools as she did at home, to make sure we had the same opportunities as any other child. She placed nothing above us.

To my mother we were entitled to the world, despite the fact that we were black, poor, and male. What mattered most to her was that we succeed in life regardless of the challenges black males face in this country. She knew that the chances of her boys ending up in prison were greater than those of the children of her white friends. She knew we were at greater risk of being killed, dropping out of high school, becoming teen fathers, or falling victim to drugs and alcohol than children from any other racial group. She knew that throughout our lives we would be the object of negative stereotypes. And she later knew about the reality of AIDS striking black men disproportionately. We were targets, and her purpose was to guide us through a potentially deadly firing range as best she could. But my mother was not alone in her determination. She was one of many women in our community who struggled, sacrificed, and fought to raise their sons to be strong, to be responsible, and to stand before the world to disprove any stereotype. They wanted their sons to be prepared to function in a world that could be hostile to them, and armed them with the will to pursue and fulfill their dreams despite the obstacles.

During my career as a broadcast journalist, I realized how news stories tend to portray one-dimensional, often negative images of black mothers. More complex and powerful stories were going untold — stories that encompassed the complexities and richness of our mothers' character and revealed the triumphs as well as the struggles they have in raising their children, particularly their sons.

In this collection of interviews, I hope to capture the true range of human experience, as well as the diversity within the black community. The mothers I met are African American, Caribbean American, Latina, Asian, and Caucasian; they are rich, middle class, working class, and poor. Sometimes the matriarch of the family is the grandmother, sometimes an aunt, a cousin, or Miss so-and-so down the street. Regardless of class, race, or family relationships, these mothers had to find ways to give their sons confidence and the ability to perform in a society that often questions them, fears them, and views them as the embodiment of America's worst pathologies. *Sacred Bond* celebrates the courage, the strength, and the resilience of these mothers in their arduous mission of raising black boys to become successful men.

In the pages ahead are the personal histories of thirty-six men of all ages, from different regions of the country and from a variety of backgrounds. As a body of work, their stories address a wide range of contemporary issues: race, class, education, family, relationships, religion, drug addiction, domestic violence, and death. But the truly valuable part of these testimonies is their emotional candor. Though the men speak only from their own experience, their words express the thoughts and feelings of many others who are unable to articulate what their mothers mean to them and the impact they have had on their lives.

The black men I interviewed for the book are all "successful." Some of them were surprised I wanted to include them, because they didn't consider themselves successful in the traditional sense of the word. I took the liberty of broadly defining successful as anyone who has been able to escape or overcome the pitfalls to which so many black men have fallen victim. This definition yielded a variety of men, from a young man working as a janitor to support his daughter, to an undercover narcotics officer, to the deputy attorney general of the United States. I found them through extensive research and the help of colleagues, friends, and friends of friends. Early on I realized I could have included hundreds. The men in the book are at various stages of their professions, some just starting out, others quite accomplished in their fields. They include high school and college students, police officers, doctors, educators, business executives, lawyers, artists, entertainers, and community activists. Their ages span six decades. Most important, these are men who have a sense of purpose that extends beyond their own success — men who are committed to their communities and to their families, and who refuse to give up on their pursuit of the American dream.

A number of those I interviewed said this was the first time they had ever talked candidly about their feelings for their mothers, and in the course of conducting the interviews some painful memories surfaced. There were times the tape recorder was turned off so they could regain their composure. They shared stories of loss, abandonment, reconciliation, and love. Much of their angst these men related directly to abandonment or rejection by their fathers, and the physical and emotional toll of their fathers' absence on their mothers. Many times during the interviews I was told "My mom was the mother and the father." I noticed that men raised in such households had a sense of responsibility and obligation toward their mothers that didn't seem as urgent in men whose fathers were present. Although the focus of this book is on the mother-son relationship, the father-son relationship — whether good or bad — obviously played an important role in these men's lives.

I also realized there are conflicting views about the bond between black men and their mothers. Many women I talked to about this project felt that black men were spoiled by their mothers, and that the maternal attachment impinges on men's relationships with other women. For their part, several men revealed their belief that women with the strength and fortitude of their mothers no longer exist. And as for the effects of their maternal attachment, the overwhelming majority of the men said their mothers have made them more sensitive people and ultimately better husbands, boyfriends, and fathers.

I was fortunate to team up with Adger W. Cowans, an award-winning photographer whose work has been exhibited in galleries and museums around the world. He brought insight, warmth, and a personal understanding of the importance of the mother-son bond. He says his own mother was the one who encouraged him and supported his becoming a photographer.

Many times during the months we worked on the project, he reiterated, "It's about the feelings." And that's exactly what his heartfelt black-and-white photographs convey.

As Adger and I were welcomed into dozens of homes, one thing was clear in the way these mothers and sons looked at each other, the way they touched, and the way they playfully interacted with one another: each woman was proud to be her son's mother, and each man was proud to be his mother's child. Some displays were subtle, some larger than life. But in each photograph, even those that capture the more strained or distant relationships, we managed to document that special connection between them.

With each story that I was told, I gained new insight into myself and my relationship with my mother. Some men's recollections reminded me that I need to be more appreciative of her, that I should call her more often, and that I should tell my mother I love her at every opportunity. Recollections of special gifts, funny moments, family outings, or memorable spankings brought back things I hadn't thought about in years. These stories made me feel thankful for the unconditional love that I and a lot of others have been given — a love that has carried us through, when so many of our brothers have been broken and lost.

Ten years have passed since the day my mother read that letter to my brother. I know she still feels the pain of his loss. I think there are times when she still questions whether she was a good mother, or if she were somehow to blame for his death, or if she could have done things differently. But I also know there is solace and resolution for my mother: She comforted Marc in his darkest moment; she nursed his sores and washed his body when others were afraid to touch him; she loved him when he needed it most; and when Marc got tired of fighting, she had the courage to tell him it was okay to let go. She fulfilled her commitment to my brother to his last breath. What more could a son ask for?

Sacred Bond is for all the mothers who believe in us, support us, and love us for everything that we are, good and bad. It is our way of giving thanks.

There is an enduring tenderness in the
love of a mother to a son that transcends
all other affections of the heart.
WASHINGTON IRVING
(1783 – 1859)

SACRED BOND

JAMES LOVE & HENRIETTA LOVE

A MOTHER'S VALOR

Most mothers instinctively protect their children from harm. Depending on the level of crime and violence in their community, how a mother protects her children and how she teaches them to protect themselves can make the difference between her children's survival and their demise. Of the men I interviewed, Chicago police officer James Love grew up in the roughest neighborhood, the Robert Taylor Homes, one of the most notorious housing projects in the country. His mother was his first line of defense against violence, gangs, and the unpredictable situations he encountered daily. Now, as an undercover narcotics officer, Love has survival skills, learned from her, that are a valuable asset in his efforts to help rid the Chicago projects of drugs. ■ His mother is employed as a maintenance worker at Johnson Publishing Company, publisher of *Ebony* and *Jet* magazines. With her impeccable style, she looks more like a woman who would organize garden parties than confront gangs, but her toughness has helped her son persevere both on and off the job. Their mother-son bond has provided ongoing support and guidance to Love, who daily lives with violence and the stress associated with it. His mother's love has given him the inspiration to overcome crises in his life and to remain steadfast in his mission to clean up the streets. For his heroism in the drug war Love has received a Medal of Valor — the highest honor a policeman can receive — but to him the only hero in his life is his mother, Henrietta Love.

JAMES LOVE
Narcotics Officer
AGE FORTY
MOTHER HENRIETTA LOVE

I was conducting search warrants in the projects where a gang called the Gangster Disciples conducted business when they ordered a contract on my life. I continued doing searches, even when I got called into the station and was told that the contract had gone into effect. I knew this wasn't a joke, but you can't be out there trying to clean up the streets if you're going to run from people.

One night I was working with two white officers and we were going into the projects. They dropped me off at this dead end area so I could walk though a viaduct into the projects. That is how we would always do it. But this time after they pulled off to get set up, a van pulls up. The cargo doors open and I'm looking at guns. Right away I'm thinking, "Oh you dummies, trying to rob a cop." Then they called me Twenty-one, which is a little tag name for undercover cops. I knew that they knew I was a cop. They told me to get in the van, and I did. They disarmed me except for a snub-nose that I keep strapped to my ankle. One of the things that you learn from the streets is to always keep talking, always have something to say to keep them off balance, to misdirect them, and that's what I did. There were three guys, two teenagers and an older guy; one of them stayed in the back of the van with me the whole time. At one point they made me lie face down in the van. I never got a chance to go for my snub.

One of the kids wanted to shoot me right there, but the adult wouldn't let him. They took me to an abandoned garage of some kind, a warehouse, and there was nowhere to run. I kept talking steady while at the same time silently asking forgiveness for everything that I ever did wrong. I kept telling myself that it was a bluff, that they were just trying to scare me. But then, I don't know why, I couldn't bet anymore and just said, "Shoot me if you're going to." And that's when the kid lit me up. I took four bullets: one above the knee, one bullet fractured my right forearm, and I took two to the sternum.

Something said fall down, play dead, and that's what I did. I had a great vest on, but it is not like television where they show someone getting shot and the guy just takes it in the vest. It hurts, and knocks the wind out of you. I never knew that I blacked out at some point until afterwards, when I got the photos of the shooting and saw that there was a pool of blood. I was like, God, I must have laid there for a while. I don't even remember that. I do remember looking around and seeing garbage everywhere and thinking, if I'm going to die, I'm going to die looking at the stars. I didn't want to die in this filth. I thought about a sergeant in the Special Forces who always used to say, "Bullets don't kill, shock kills you. No matter what, be calm." I remember sitting up in the dirt, my bright yellow shirt was red, my blue jeans were soaked with blood. I took my shoelaces out and used my mouth to tie them around my arm and leg to make tourniquets, and I got up and started walking.

This was a July night. It was hot. The windows were open in the buildings around me and nobody answered my screams. This was at one o'clock in the morning. I left a trail of blood about four blocks long. That's how the police knew every house I went to and were able to find the warehouse where I got shot.

I didn't know where I was. I remember there was a guy going to the trunk of a car with some fishing gear. I really wasn't hurting anymore, I was just tired. I wanted to go to sleep. But I kept my badge in my crotch, and I remember taking my badge out as I walked towards this guy. I told him I was a police officer. "I've been shot," I said. "I don't know where I am, call 911." The guy's eyes just got big as saucers, and he backed away from me and ran into a house. At that point I was like, forget it, I am tired. I remember trying to stand up against a fence and the next thing I know, I had slid down into a seated position. I was laying on my side and I could see a woman running from the same house towards me with a bunch of towels. That woman cradled me and it felt like my mother was there holding me. I was okay then. And she kept telling me you're going to be all right — all those things your mother said to you when you were a kid. "You're going to be okay," she said. At that moment it didn't matter whether I lived or died, because I wasn't alone.

I could hear the sirens coming, but by then I was in noogy-noogy land. I was so worried about the precinct notifying my mother that I'd been shot. I thought, "That woman's going to come in here hysterical, with rollers in her hair and house slippers. They're going to have to sedate her." They had me in intensive care, and she walked in and I looked up, and there is my mom in a two-piece pants suit, makeup, hair done, and this was about four o'clock in the

morning. She was dressed to the nines. I'm hooked up to all these machines and I'm just looking at her, and I smiled at her and she smiled back.

"I knew you were going to be okay," she said, "so I figured I might as well dress up for the occasion." Grown men had been sobbing in the trauma unit because I was such a bloody mess. But my mother leaned over my hospital bed and said, "God spared you for a reason." Just hearing her words gave me a new sense of responsibility.

About four or five days later I signed myself out of the hospital, and my mother and sister picked me up. I remember when my mom put me in the car, she was talking to me about life, about God. I always concerned myself with getting from point A to point B and had already begun thinking of twenty different things I had to do; but listening to her, I could actually feel the heat of the sun on my face. I let the window down. I could feel the wind. By the time we made the turn to go down the block of the neighborhood, I could actually smell the fresh grass. I had never paid any attention to those things before, and my mother pointed them out to me.

At the same time I was shot, my father lost a lung to cancer. So he was in one bedroom, I was in the adjacent bedroom, and my mom ran back and forth between us. I've got all these wounds and dressings that have to be cleaned and changed, and the same thing with my dad. She took care of us both and never complained. And she still worked every day. After I recovered, my mother didn't want me to go back to the job, but she understood why I had to do it. I had to prove that the monkey wasn't on my back. So I went back to buying dope with her blessing.

The police got the two juveniles the same night I got shot. They got the adult a couple of days later, and he was later sentenced to eighty-five years in prison. The juveniles pled out: the shooter got twenty-five years and the other one eighteen years.

If it wasn't for my mother, I could have been one of those kids. I grew up in the Robert Taylor Homes, and there were a lot of gang bangers and drug dealers. My mother didn't play that. On a couple of occasions these gang bangers tried to recruit my older brother. One time I got him out of being recruited and the other time my mother did. They were just about to start initiations and my mother got word that they had him down at the playground. She went down there and walked right through them, and these guys were hardcore gang bangers. She got my brother and told him first what they weren't going to do to him, then she turned around and told the gang bangers what they weren't going to do to her or her son. I was with her and said, "Are you sure you are thinking, Ma? You are going to get us all killed." But she continued to tell them what she would do if they ever put a hand on her son again. She took my brother by the hand and brought him on upstairs, and the gangs never messed with him again. Never.

My mother was hands-on. I'm telling you, my mother could beat your ass. One time when the Isley Brothers were hot, I wanted to go over to this girl's house to listen to the new album I had. So I asked my mother if I could go; I was about fifteen. "Don't you go out of this house," she told me. As soon as I heard her get into bed, I got my albums, tiptoed out the door, and went by the girl's house. I impressed her with my music and came on back home. I knew if I used the back gate the latch would make noise, so I climbed over the neighbor's fence. That's how slick I was, didn't make a sound and came in through the back door. The second I pushed the back door open, that woman beat my ass. In total darkness. I didn't know what the hell happened to me. A light never came on; all you could hear was "Ooh, ow, ooh, ow, ooh, ow." Never turned on a single light. "Now go to bed," she said. That was my last whupping, because it was the last time I tried that lady. To this day, we laugh about it. It's one of the family jokes. Mama can beat your ass in total darkness. But I can't remember a time she wasn't there for us.

My mother grew up in Mississippi working the fields. She had to quit school, because when harvesttime came all the kids had to help my grandfather on the farm; so she never made it past the eighth grade. Her way of providing for her children was also through backbreaking labor. During the times when people didn't have floor buffers, you had women on their knees buffing. My mother was one of them. And I never realized that. So here's a woman who was getting up in the projects at four-thirty in the morning, pitch black, going to work as a maid. Ten hours a day working, and the only thing she had to eat was crackers. But she never complained, not once.

Education was always the biggest thing that she pushed, schoolwork, schoolwork, schoolwork, because she knew that that was the only way we would be able to compete in the world. So that was her driving force, that her kids weren't going to go through what she did. She was never in a position where she could help us with our homework or things like that. If she received a letter or something, she'd say, "I can't find my glasses. Can you read this letter for me?" She didn't want me to know that she really couldn't read the letter.

But no matter what, my mother can find something to be positive about, even in a hurricane. That's just the way she is. Mama would give you one of her little sayings: "Your heart is just like a sprained ankle right now, but it's going to be okay." No matter what, she's always pushing. Every time you thought life was over and you couldn't go any further, she has always been there with some encouragement.

Around the time I found out that the contract was out on me, there were a lot of other things going on in my life. My wife and I were splitting up. Even though we were already separated, I asked her to hold off on the divorce because I just couldn't deal with it at the time. Also, the reality about my son set in, that I wouldn't be able to see him when I wanted, and he would not always have a father around who was hands-on. I was so despondent that I called my mother from a pay phone. I called her to say I was sorry that I had failed. I told her that I just wanted to die. My mother said to hold on, your father wants to talk to you. So I talked with my dad, and I didn't know it but my mother was already on her way. She knew I was near the expressway, on Eighty-seventh Street. She drove all around until she found me. "If you die," she said, "then I'm going to die with you." With those words all thoughts of ever wanting to leave this earth left me. So now, regardless of how despondent I may get, I know my mother is depending on me the way I depended on her for so long. She's my hero. I can receive all the awards, all the accolades, but none of them mean anything in comparison to her. What I do, I do because she was there for me. Maybe if the kid who shot me had a mother like mine, he wouldn't be sitting where he is today.

DAVID A. PATERSON & PORTIA EMILY PATERSON

Ｎew York state senator David Paterson was raised in a protected, middle-class community. His mother didn't have to fear gangs or random violence, but she had an even more immediate concern, one unlike anyone else's in this collection of interviews: her son is legally blind. He lost 90 percent of his eyesight during infancy when scar tissue caused by a rare condition blocked his vision. But Portia Paterson had her own vision: her son would never be handicapped by his disability. In her efforts to make him strong and build his confidence, Portia Paterson not only protected her firstborn child, she also pushed him. ▪ Her desire for her son to be treated the same as anyone else had an impact: Paterson is now considered one of the rising stars in New York politics. His stellar career parallels that of his father, Basil Paterson, a lawyer and former New York state senator. Now for the second time in history, the Paterson name has been mentioned in discussions about the next black candidate for mayor of New York City. Paterson's mother relinquished her career as an educator to support her husband's political aspirations, and with the same selfless determination, she urged her son to fully experience life. ▪ But there was a consequence to her unique blend of vigilance and tough love: Paterson says he never received the kind of nurturing, "motherly" love he expected. At the same time, however, he recognizes that his mother gave him what she felt he needed, and that, ultimately, his relationship with his mother contributed significantly to his ability to succeed.

DAVID A. PATERSON
State Senator
AGE FORTY-FOUR
MOTHER PORTIA EMILY PATERSON

——

My loss of eyesight happened when I was somewhere from six to nine months old. My mother said she had a funny feeling about me from the day I was born. I always tell her I had a funny feeling about *her* since the day I was born. I was one of the first blind students in the public school system in Hempstead, Long Island. Most blind students were sent to special schools at the time, but my mother wanted me to be independent. She would have to come in to school and be the sheriff. Their idea was to push me through; my mother's idea was different: I should learn what everyone else learns.

When she first sent me to kindergarten, the teacher did not want to take me. She said to give her two weeks to get the other students settled down, then they'd be ready for me. My mother and an actress named Billie Allen Henderson, who lived in Hempstead, went back to the school, and apparently they performed – they went off. Only after the fight did the teacher let me in, but then because it was the law. I never thought of myself like James Meredith or somebody else, who desegregated public schools, but apparently there was a dispute about me being admitted. My mother was right in the middle of it. My father was always supportive, but he was busy building a law practice that was a distance away. My mother really carried the hatchet.

My mother told me later that she used to let me walk home from school by myself when I got to the age that the other kids did. But she was out there watching, although she didn't want me to know. When someone told me they just saw my mother pass by, I thought they meant she was driving. But I later found out what she did was walk, so she could see me without me seeing her. She really didn't want to follow me at all, because she thought I could make it. She had taught me how to travel a little differently than other kids. For example, she couldn't say to me, "Look both ways." Instead she'd say, "Only cross the streets if you see that the cars are stopped." She knew

I couldn't tell the difference between a red light and a green light, so she taught me a way to get home that she thought would work a hundred percent of the time. But she said she still felt guilty. That's why she was out there.

My mother kept forcing me into different areas. One thing that she may not have done, though, is make it clear to me that I had limitations. Maybe she didn't want me to feel that I had any, but to some degree this created a problem as I got older. When I ran into my limitations, I didn't know what to do. "You mean I can't play baseball?" I'd question. "No, if you don't see this ball coming at you at sixty miles an hour, you can't play," I was told. I think my expectations were built up, and when they weren't met, my reaction was to go the other way: "Now I can't do anything." I think it is important to make a person feel positive, but with the understanding that at times they'll have issues to address a little differently than other people. My mother treated me as if I had no disability at all. She was tough because everyone in the neighborhood coddled me, especially the mothers. The girls in my class used to pick me up and walk me to school. I don't think my mother realized that's what they were doing. They were going out of their way to get me and to walk me back home just because they wanted to do it. I was always popular and basically gracious, so people would help me. My father was that way too, very sensitive toward me.

When I was about fourteen, my mother and I had a confrontation because she did finally acknowledge my disability. She sent me to a mobility course. Each weekend they would take a lot of blind kids and teach them how to cook; teach them how to sew. But I was pissed! I was raised as if I had no problem. I couldn't explain to my friends where I was going on Saturdays, so I lied to them. I told them I was going to see a sick relative every weekend. I fought going to that course, because there I was, in with the blind kids from the special schools, and they were almost helpless. And I hate to say this, but I had the same anger I think some successful black people who were raised in white neighborhoods have against poorer blacks. They think, "These people are bringing me down." When they called me "blind" in that course, I thought, they're not talking about me, they are talking about themselves; these are the people who are causing me the problem; they're helpless; they can't do anything. I thought of myself as different. I was really hostile to them, and they didn't like me very much either. There was another kid who probably had the same vision as I had, and he thought he would teach us how to bounce a basketball. Well, I had played basketball. So I bounced the ball and then deliberately threw it hard at the kid. I almost knocked him over. I was really angry, and my mother was forcing me to go.

13

My brother and I had made a five-dollar bet about which of us dared jump out of the second-story window of the house. Well, the first time he bet me, I didn't jump. Next time I was so mad, because I felt that my masculinity was being taken away by this class, that I came home, walked into his room, and said to him, "Forget the five dollars. I'm jumping now." I jumped out the window. I didn't see that there was a little ledge that protruded, so when I jumped, the ledge flipped me over. Instead of going down feet first, I went down head first. Fortunately my hand went out in time. I ended up in the hospital with a broken wrist, trying to explain why this happened. My mother sat down with me and we had a very frank conversation. What I remember most of all was her listening. She didn't lecture. I told her I didn't like going to this mobility course. Well, I'll tell you what, I needed to go more than ever now that I had both a sight problem and a broken arm. My mother said, "You felt you had to pretend to your friends that you don't have a sight problem. I thought that going to this course would be a message to your friends that you need a little help every once in a while."

I don't think I was buying her answer, but she brought to my attention that I had complained about an incident with other kids. A group of us were going somewhere on the bus. The other kids got on and put their tokens in the box. I couldn't find the box. I was holding everyone up. The bus driver started yelling at me, and one of my friends in a disgusted way came over to me, snatched the token out of my hand, and dropped it in the box. I felt humiliated. I felt that my friends shouldn't have left me standing there like that, that they didn't care about me.

I do remember raising this with my mother. "You see, you're sending the world different messages," she said. "Some-times you want to be independent, then all of a sudden you want people to help you. You've got to be consistent. Even around here. Half the time you don't want anyone to touch you, you don't want people to hold you when you walk down steps, but then when you fall and hurt yourself you wonder how come no one helped you." What she was doing was challenging me to work the problem out. She was challenging me to face up to the problem myself.

My mother didn't send me back to the course. I don't think she ever made me go to another until I went to Syracuse University for a summer before I started college at Columbia. Each year in the summer the state would have a mobility program for blind students. My mother wanted me to go, and this time I didn't object. I took that course, and I went on to two years of college at Columbia University.

Then a strange thing happened to me. A man who lived in Hempstead and was a friend of the family ran a catering service during the summer. He asked me and another guy to recruit people for the catering service. He hired all of the guys we referred to him, all of them except me. It was just like my first day in kindergarten. My mother went with me to the place to talk to him on the day everyone started working. He told my mother that these were the people he hired for today, and he was going to keep them on for a couple of weeks and then see what happens. He never hired me. About two or three weeks into the summer, when normally I'd be in summer school, I had no job and no one to hang out with because I got this job for all my friends. And to top it off, he tried to make it up to my family by hiring my underage brother. I was pissed, I was just pissed at life. I've always thought that's the summer I would have started a drug problem, but I was so overprotected I couldn't find the drugs. I was totally destroyed. One day I went in and confronted my mother. "Don't you understand," I said to her, "he didn't hire me because of my sight problem! That's why he didn't hire me. They'd rather break the law and hire someone underage before they'll hire me!" I went off. I later found out from a friend of hers that the conversation really upset her. My mother never spoke to the caterer's family again.

I couldn't get over that summer. I went back to Columbia and basically flunked out. The only reason they didn't throw me out was that the semester before, I was on the dean's list. My feeling after not getting this job was, Why should I go to school? No one will ever hire me. That's where my mother came in. "So your impression is, somebody mistreats you so you're going to take your toys and run home?" She was saying that I was reacting like a child. "I'm not saying you are a child," she said. "But that's your conduct. What you've got to do is get your conduct to coincide with your age." She suggested that I finish college. "You know you can do that. Then go out and get a job. And no one will help you, just go get one." In other words, go fight that battle. Then she said, "David, about what that man did to you, you're right, he probably did discriminate against you. But you knew it all along. Why didn't you raise hell? Where were you?"

I then realized I did nothing but internalize it. After that conversation, I went back to college and finished. I then took on the problem. I went to work for a credit union. People fought there every day. I remember the first person I ever saw as a client. He said, "Can't they get somebody out here who can see?" I had my glasses on, but when I read I have to put my face right against the paper. "I can read this application," I said to him. "I'm a graduate of Columbia University. I daresay that I would understand it better than the other people that work here, and better than yourself. But if you don't want me to do it, fine!" I just threw the application at him. "Well, no, no," he said. "I'm just a little concerned." But I found out that as soon as I stood up to him he felt better. And I certainly did. That came from my mom, that kind of in-your-face stuff you have to do once in a while.

After I became a state senator, a fund-raiser was being held for me in Hempstead, and would you believe, the guy who set me on this path, the man who wouldn't hire me for a summer job, was there. He came up to me and said, "We always knew you were going to be good. From when you were a little kid we thought you were going to be very successful." I know I shouldn't have done this, but there were six or seven people around, and I said to him, "Listen, all I want you to know is I have a list. A list of a lot of people to thank and a shorter list of people not to thank. I just hope you know which list you're on." I felt good. I know it's wrong. I went back and told my mother what had happened. She said, "David, after all of your successes these days, I think for you to go back and take a shot at him like that is cruel."

"I'm sorry, but that's how I feel," I told her. "I wanted him to know it. I can forgive that kind of thing, but that man would not even let me try. He wouldn't even let me sit down and explain to him how I can put an apple in a box for a bunch of kids, and then he had the audacity to hire my brother. I would have reported him to the Department of Labor if it wasn't my brother he hired." Then my mother thought about it for a minute and said, "Actually, I think it's really funny."

I think my mother would be surprised to know what an influence she has been in my life. She is the one who pushed me. I'd say she was the primary motivation for my desire to succeed, my ambition. I don't think that I would be a state senator or a minority leader without my mother. She was tough on me. But I think she always knew that people's hearts would go out to me because of my disability. I think she thought what I needed was not help as much as confidence. Her whole objective, even if it wasn't obvious to me, was to build my confidence. It was hard, but in the end it made me stronger.

KEVIN FOSTER, CLAUDETTE ABDUL-ALEEM & AUREOLA PETRUS

19

When a mother finds herself unable to protect her children, members of the extended family become a crucial resource. Most of the men I spoke to had depended on the support of other women in the family – aunts, and especially grandmothers – at some point during their formative years. But among those men, Kevin Foster needed his grandmother's support the most urgently. She stepped in at a critical moment and offered a safe haven from domestic violence. ▪ Initially, Foster was reluctant to do the interview because he didn't want his mother to feel unappreciated for all she has done for him. Though his relationship with his mother remains close, he considers his grandmother the primary female figure in his life. Granama Orla, as he affectionately calls her, protected Foster and his twin brother when his mother no longer could. His grandmother's home, and her mere presence, became a constant source of stability and inspiration. The financial and personal sacrifices she made for her grandson assured that Foster would achieve his goal of becoming a lawyer. He is now an attorney for Price Waterhouse, a Washington, D.C.–based international accounting firm. ▪ Although Foster's mother couldn't flee the abuse herself, she had the courage to let her sons go to a place where she knew that they could live without fear of harm. The grandmother-grandson relationship, in the end, was vital in providing physical and emotional relief to the boys and a link between family members as they weathered a time of crisis.

KEVIN FOSTER
Banking Attorney
AGE THIRTY
MOTHER CLAUDETTE ABDUL-ALEEM
GRANDMOTHER AUREOLA "ORLA" PETRUS

———

My mother is a real friend. There were times when I would feel depressed and there wasn't anyone that I could turn to but my mother. I can tell her every intimate detail of my life and she'll understand it and won't be judgmental. I'm very close to her, but it is my grandmother who I look to as my mother. She is the one who saved me and my twin brother from the abuse we experienced.

We called her Granama Orla when we were little. She is a strong woman from St. Croix in the Virgin Islands. She came here as a young woman in the early twenties, leaving my mother and her sister in the Virgin Islands for about two years until she could send for them. She came here with just a high school diploma, started out cleaning toilets, and went to night school. She became a nurse's aide and then worked her way through nursing school. My grandmother is the type who when you meet her may seem a little tough. Her feathers are ruffled easily. That's just the way she is, but you have to know that she doesn't mean anything by it; she loves you to death nonetheless.

Growing up with my mother was good for the most part, but I can't escape that I had a stepfather who was an alcoholic. When it was bad, it was nightmarish; that's the only way I can describe it. He was physically abusive, usually at night. He would come home drunk, and if he wasn't hitting my mother he'd be hitting my brother and me. He took punishment to the extreme, using wires, electrical cords, things like that. If he was beating us and it got out of hand, my mother would try to shield us. But she couldn't stop it. We learned how to tiptoe, because he never beat us at the moment we did something wrong or he felt we did something. He would just say, "I will see you tonight, young man." That meant that some time before we went to bed, or even after we were already asleep, he would drag one of us out for a beating. At times we would try to sneak into bed early, hoping that maybe he would have forgotten. Or maybe he would have had too much to drink and would just come home and fall out. That only happened a couple of times. Even then, he would get us the next morning. As we got older, my mother started defending us. She would physically block him or hold him at bay. But there was only so much she could do, because she was also a victim of his abuse. I didn't think she had the guts to leave at that point. My mother was very religious and still is, so getting a divorce wasn't an option for her then. She didn't divorce him until I went to college.

We thought our stepfather was really our father until we were about four or five. We were coming home from some kind of gathering. We were walking home from the bus stop and he was drunk and carrying on. We got into the house and he started harassing me and my brothers. Even though he harassed my little brother too, he would always give my twin brother, Keith, and me a little extra. Once, he came into the bedroom and said to us, "You know what? I'm not even your father." That's all he said. It was a relief to us that we weren't part of this monster. But then the flip side was that my younger brother had to come to terms with the fact that he was the progeny of this man.

My grandmother was always calling child protective services. I remember once when we were in the third grade people came to school asking us questions. I remember being happy because we thought, this is going to put an end to it. But no action was taken. There was a time when my grandmother even fought with my stepfather. One Christmas Eve my grandmother was visiting, and she got into an argument with my stepfather about how he was treating us. The argument got so heated, the next thing I knew he was trying to throw her out of the apartment. I remember she picked up the Christmas tree, one of those tabletop Christmas trees, and she threw it at him

to stave him off. She had these leather boots that zipped up and I remember one of them coming off. We all ran downstairs to take refuge in my aunt's apartment one floor below us. There were times when we stayed with my aunt for a week.

When my twin brother and I were about twelve, our stepfather threatened us for the last time. We were fed up and couldn't take the abuse anymore, so instead of going home after school we took the bus to the library. My grandmother didn't get home from work till about six-thirty, then we headed to her house. She said we could stay with her as along as we wanted. Our stepfather threatened to come get us, but for whatever reason, he didn't. I remember that my mother was so sad.

When we got to my grandmother's house, I finally had freedom. With my grandmother there was this feeling, this luxury, of being a child again, of not having to worry about anything. My grandmother wasn't a nurturing

woman, so there weren't a lot of touchy-feely type things, but she cared deeply and she spoiled us. The attention she gave us was a bone of contention in the family, too. They felt that she favored me and my brother over all of her other grandchildren. She said the reason she did was that we didn't have a father to pick up the slack.

After about a month or two with my grandmother, I went back to live with my mother because I felt sorry for her. Not necessarily for what she was going through, because I felt like that was her choice. I felt like she could have left if she really wanted to get rid of him. I felt bad because I thought she felt that her children had abandoned her. At first my stepfather didn't bother me. We wouldn't even speak unless he wanted me to run to the store to buy his cigarettes or his beer or to run errands for him. He would say snide or threatening things but never followed up. Then one day a group of my mother's friends and their kids were at the house. I either said something or did something that he didn't like, or maybe I didn't move quickly enough when he was prodding me to do something. He simply said, "I'll see you tonight." Right then and there I told my mother, "I just can't go through that again." I packed my bags and left. I had been back less than a year. My mother told me again that she understood.

I loved my mother all along, but I was mad at her. I was mad at her that she wouldn't take action, not just for my sake, but for her own sake too. I just didn't understand how she could endure the beatings. I guess maybe she loved him, even though I can't fathom how anybody could and how she stayed. I know to a large degree it was fear. Maybe she felt she wouldn't find anyone else and feared being alone.

After I returned to my grandmother I spoke to my mother almost every day. And we continued to see our mother. We would either visit when my stepfather wasn't home, or we wouldn't speak to him if he was. We still went to the same church as my mother. There wasn't any type of legal custody arrangement; my mother said it was best for my brother and me to live with my grandmother and accepted it. I think her biggest sacrifice was letting us go so that we could have a better life, a safer life. From that point on my grandmother was a tremendous force in my life. She has been a strong example for us.

My grandmother worked at the same hospital for thirty-five years, retiring two years ago as one of the top administrative nurses. I remember she was working on her master's degree in nursing. She really worked hard and did it all. She rose at five-thirty every morning and was in bed by nine every night as long as I can remember. She'd always get to work forty-five minutes early every day, because she could never be late to work. She never paid a bill late. That's just the type of woman she is, by the book, and that's how she raised us. I'm grateful for the strict West Indian upbringing now. It was hard, but it kept me out of trouble.

At every stage in my life my grandmother has always been there pushing me. And she made many financial sacrifices to send me to a private high school, to college, even to law school. She just worked hard, and she saved, saved, saved. She was able to help me out in ways that my mother couldn't. I feel blessed to have such a grandmother. To a certain extent I think my mother felt as if she missed out on raising me and my twin, even though she still had two other kids at home. We were her twins, her firstborn. But I think in her mind she was doing what she thought she had to do. I don't think my mother realized how bad it was, because I remember talking to her maybe three or four years ago and she asked me, "Was it really that bad?" I think she was dealing with her own trauma so much that maybe she didn't realize how bad it was. Or maybe she just chose to forget.

Sacred Bond

BILL DUKE & ETHEL LOUISE DUKE

NO EXCUSE FOR FAILURE

There comes a time when every black man in America confronts racism, whether it's in the form of being followed in a department store, or called "nigger," or actually assaulted. As hard as our mothers try to shield us, racism has left its indelible imprint on each of us. In actor/director Bill Duke's case, the unbridled racism his mother, Ethel Louise Duke, had to endure in a segregated South of the early 1900s put his own hardships in perspective. His mother's hard-earned wisdom gave Duke the tenacity to cope and to succeed in one of the most competitive, racially stratified industries in this country. ▪ Duke's accomplished career in Hollywood, as an actor and a director, spans several decades and encompasses both film and television. He appeared in such movies as *Predator*, *American Gigolo*, and *Car Wash*. He directed the feature films *A Rage in Harlem*, *Sister Act 2*, *Hoodlum*, and *Deep Cover*, as well as countless television episodes. He is also the author of two books. He attributes his longevity in the entertainment business to the power of people like his father, the late William Henry Duke Sr., and his mother, two people who never settled for anything less than equality. ▪ I went with Duke to his mother's home during one of his trips to the East Coast. He sat with his mother in her bedroom and listened to her attentively, as if no one else was around. Though she has been weakened by diabetes and heart disease, he continues to draw strength from his mother — a woman who never tolerated racism as an excuse for failure.

BILL DUKE
Author/Actor/Director
AGE FIFTY-FOUR
MOTHER ETHEL LOUISE DUKE

When I was eleven or twelve, I was beaten up by four young white men. I was coming from a social event at church. My sister and I were walking down the street and these guys said, "Where you niggers going?" We kept on walking, and when they caught up with us I decided to defend my sister. They proceeded to kick my butt. I was very upset by the ordeal, and when I got home I told my mother that it wasn't over, that I was going to get them. I couldn't just let it go. It wasn't fair, I hadn't done anything to them. But my mother talked to me very seriously about life's realities. She agreed that what had happened was not fair, but she explained about the fifties, who the people were and the consequences of my actions if I were to retaliate. She wouldn't let me go, and I resented her for that. Even at eleven or twelve, I felt that she was taking my manhood away. I didn't have only physical bruises from the beatings, but I had inner kinds of bruises too. She was taking away my identity by not letting me go back. I know she saw the pain I was going through, and she knew I didn't understand her decision, but she believed there would be a time when I would.

From a young person's perspective, it was hard to understand my parents. They came from the South, my mother from West Point, Mississippi, and my father from Orange, Virginia.

They both migrated to Poughkeepsie for work. My sister and I thought they were mean or hard, but these were people who had lived through the Depression. They had seen black folks lynched. People who lived in the segregated South in those days had seen atrocities and indignities that we can't even begin to think about today. My mother remembers walking down the street with her parents on the way to church. At that time they didn't have cement sidewalks or a street, they had wooden sidewalks and dirt streets. It was raining, and my mother and her family were walking in one direction and some white folks were walking in the other direction to their own church. My mother's family all just stepped off the sidewalk into the mud. They looked down so they wouldn't look the white folks in the eyes as they passed. Then they got back up on the sidewalk and continued on to church.

They were able to survive those indignities and maintain a sense of self and a sense of pride. These are survivors, people who made sacrifices so that their children wouldn't have to look down for anyone. That's what my mother passed on to me, a sense of what I call generational responsibility. They endured so their children could have a better life. My father worked three and four jobs so that my sister and I could have the education that he and my mother never had; and to buy a house so he could have a yard and could tell somebody to get the hell off his property.

My mother and father always told us that they never wanted us to make the same mistakes they made in life. They never followed their dreams. They had a second- and a third-grade education and had to settle for certain things. My mother worked as a domestic, and many years later she went back to school and became a practical nurse. So my mother's priority was for us to go to school and get out of that town. She never allowed us to let anybody set limits for us. And we were not allowed to use race as an excuse for failure. She said, "You're only going to be limited by your ability, not by your ethnicity." If we ever came in talking about how unfair life was, my mother would not tolerate it. It was not something you were even allowed to discuss. It was obvious that life is not fair. My parents had seen lynchings and so many things go down in the South, they figured that the folks up north had it pretty easy. So my sister and I were expected to achieve. It wasn't an option.

We didn't have the choice of not going to college, and we didn't really have the choice of what we wanted to be. My mother said, you're going to be a doctor, simple as that. Not, do you want to be a doctor? The attitude was you're going to go to medical school and we're going to save the money to help you. When I realized I had no talent for it, my mother said the next best thing was to be a teacher. When I told her I wanted to be an actor, it was horrible. It was devastating to them because they had gone through so much just trying to survive. They couldn't understand why someone who had gone to college, someone who could do something that would guarantee him a lifestyle that they could never dream of, would throw it away on something so foolhardy. When they said follow your dreams, they meant follow your dreams within the context of some practicality, not some fool-ishness. But they were the first ones there when I faltered, just as they were there when I started having success as an actor. Their commitment to me went beyond what they wanted me to be; they were committed to my happiness.

When I was on Broadway in *Ain't Supposed to Die a Natural Death*, written by Melvin Van Peebles and directed by the great Gilbert Moses, what I was doing became real to my parents. It ran on Broadway for a year. I got them transportation to New York and third row center seats. Two weeks later they brought the whole church down to see me. It was one of the proudest moments of my life — the proudest moment, actually. I think it was one of the proudest of their lives also. They understood that even though I didn't go into a profession they wanted, I had inherited their tenacity and spirit.

My mother used to come out to L.A. all the time, but she doesn't like to fly and she's been in and out of a wheelchair. I try to get home as often as I can. She's a diabetic and has arthritis. She recently had a second heart attack, but she is doing okay now. I am somewhat of a health nut and I try to pass on my knowledge of nutrition to her, but it is met with resistance. For about a year and a half I had nurses restrict her diet, and one time while they were cleaning her room they found Hostess Twinkies wrappers under her bed. Somebody was smuggling in food. It's hard to convince an eighty-five-year-old woman to do anything. She says to me, "If you make it past seventy, then we can talk." I give her my love and support in every way, but my mother does exactly what she wants. She's got to go on her own journey in the ways she chooses to go.

Her strength comes from her unfaltering belief. Through it she has an incredible insight into people and a sense of the future that my sister and I don't have. We have always relied on my mother's wisdom that everything was going to be okay. She can see things and feel things; stuff that we cannot see, she believes in. That old time stuff, that enabled those folks to sit down, protest, and get beaten. That stuff that enabled them to work for somebody else and hum a happy tune. It's hard to describe what it is, but it's like they just knew a better day was coming. There's a certain strength of purpose and self-assurance. You'd see these women leave their houses at five or six o'clock in the morning and get back around four in the afternoon. After cleaning white folks' houses they would then be up until midnight cooking meals for their own families, cleaning their own houses, helping their own children with homework. I feel strongly about my mother and about that generation. I wish that people would understand the sacrifices these folks made, because they're fading from the scene. There's a certain thing you see in their eyes, a certain strength, a certain confidence. I'm not being dramatic when I say that what they have given me is a debt I cannot repay.

JACK O'KELLEY III & MAXINE HAITH O'KELLEY

Like Bill Duke, Jack "Rusty" O'Kelley III was raised by a woman whose experiences in the segregated South had a major impact on how she raised her son. But O'Kelley grew up in a different era, one in which issues such as family, class, and privilege had as much to do with a person's identity as his color. And no one talked more pointedly about the struggle with his own identity than O'Kelley — a struggle that his mother, more than anyone else, helped him win. ▪ O'Kelley showed me photographs of his family that included generations of accomplished professionals. His father, the late Jack O'Kelley Jr., was a prominent elected official in North Carolina. His mother, Maxine Haith O'Kelley — a prominent political and civic leader in her own right — was an associate superintendent of schools. Both his parents served on numerous boards and commissions in North Carolina and nationally. In keeping with family tradition, O'Kelley is now a corporate lawyer in the Washington, D.C., office of Sullivan & Cromwell. He also serves as president of the Yale Law School Association of Washington, D.C., and is a member of the national governing board of the Yale Law School Association. ▪ O'Kelley's mother is the force behind her son's desire to achieve, and his ability to feel good about himself. With his mother's guidance, O'Kelley has developed a sense of pride in himself, his heritage, and above all, his race.

JACK O'KELLEY III
Corporate Lawyer
AGE THIRTY
MOTHER MAXINE HAITH O'KELLEY

———

Only in America would my mother be considered black. She has light brown hair, now slightly graying. Her lips are thin. She has beautiful green eyes and translucent white skin. My mother looks like a white woman. Though she never tried to pass as white, there were times she thought about it, and many members of her family actually did pass. But my mother was always proud of being black; she never wanted to be anything other. A white man once asked her, "How are you black?" She simply said, "I choose to be."

Occasionally she would let people assume she was white. She would if she wanted to see a movie that wasn't playing at the colored movie theater. Once she left her coat inside the white theater and had to tell her father. My grandfather yelled at her and gave her a whipping. He reminded her that everyone in town knew she was Claude Haith's daughter and that she was colored. But she continued to test the limits. She and a brown-skinned friend of hers would get a drink of water while in town, and one of the water fountains would say "colored," the other would say "white." My mother would drink out of the white water fountain and her friend out of the colored fountain. She would look over and say, "Hey, is there Pepsi-Cola coming out of there? It says colored." We think that's funny today, but that could have put her in jail in the South during the 1930s and '40s.

When my parents were first married, in the fifties, my mother had to carry identification showing that she was black. When they traveled together, people assumed they were an interracial couple, which in some states was illegal. When they drove to Washington, as they frequently did, it appeared they were breaking the law when they went through Virginia. If my mother hadn't carried identification they could have been arrested.

My mother's experience with race affected me tremendously, because throughout her life some whites made bigoted comments about black people directly to her, unaware that she was black. Through personal experience, she knew how differently people were treated because of race. She would say to me, "I know that white people are treated better than blacks, because when I'm treated as white it's better than when I'm treated as a black person." So she had the ammunition of her experience to tell me, "You will work harder than the other kids because it's the only way you're going to succeed."

My father died of a heart attack when I was fifteen. The day he died my mother took over. There was no power vacuum. She immediately began running things. She walked out of the hospital, and on the ride home she cried and sobbed some, but she looked me straight in the eyes and said, "We will get through this." She immediately started planning and making phone calls. She never lost control. She knew it was up to her to make sure that the plans she and my father had set for me were carried out.

My mother was a strict disciplinarian. If I even thought of putting forth less than a one-hundred-percent effort, I was disciplined for it. Failure was not an option. I had to succeed or I was out of the house. It was either play by her rules or support myself, and there was no testing her. The times I tried, disciplinary action would follow. I would get my hand, my butt, or my mouth hit. I remember when I was in high school, I back-talked her one morning at breakfast. She had asked me to take out the garbage and I forgot to do it.

"Why didn't you take out the garbage?" she said.

"I forgot," I told her.

"Well," she said, "that's not good enough."

"I'll do it! Durn it, I'll do it!" I didn't even say "damn." I said "durn," but I raised my voice at her. She just looked at me and said, "Give me the keys to your car." It was almost eight, and I had to be at school by eight-thirty.

"How am I going to get to school?" I said.

"That's your problem," she said, cool as ice. "And if you're late, I'll beat your butt."

"It's my car," I said defiantly.

"Oh no," she said. "It's my car. I paid for the car, I pay for the insurance. Give me the keys." So I gave them to her and started walking to school. She never gave in. The best way to describe my mother is "The Iron Lady in the Silk Suit." She is a very businesslike, very stately southern woman. In her silk suit, she looks like the classic southern lady. But don't mess with her; she will get you, one way or another. And she will tell you she is going to get you, too.

There was a period in high school that I resented being black. My parents moved largely in white social circles. They were public figures in the community and in the state, and were invited to things and did things that most other blacks didn't do. It gave me

a lot of privilege, and consequently, other black kids didn't quite know how to accept me. They teased me, which I resented. I knew I was black, but I didn't identify myself with them or with their issues. I took on the attitude that I was different.

My mother was very concerned that I didn't relate with black people. She'd ask me all the time, "Why don't you have black friends? Why do you always hang out with only white kids?" I had three black friends and all of us were in advanced placement courses at school, which further segregated us from other black students. I was friendly with some others but they weren't my good friends. A lot of the other black kids felt, Rusty's smarter; Rusty has more money; Rusty's parents do this and that. In high school kids can be cruel, and the white kids were always more accepting of me. I would go over their houses to hang out, and that just put a bigger wedge between me and other black kids. Being in a white environment was comfortable and easy. I would even go on vacation with white families.

When I began thinking about college, my mother suggested Hampton University. I said, "I don't want to go to a black college." I didn't think Hampton carried the same prestige as Wake Forest or Brown, the schools I was considering. "It's your family school," she said. "You'll be the third generation to go there."

I protested and protested and fought and fought, until my mother finally told me, you are going to Hampton because you need to realize you're black. I think she was so insistent because she had a fundamental belief that in hard times, you need to have black friends to stand by you as well. She had seen, through her experience growing up, that black people will stick with each other in times of adversity. She wanted me to have friends who had similar experiences and understood what it meant to

be black in America. Because no matter how sympathetic a white person is, they can never understand what it's like to be called "nigger."

Ultimately I never got to make the decision about where I was going to college. My mother told me, "Hampton is what I am going to pay for; if you can figure out a way to pay for college yourself you can go wherever you want. But as long as I'm paying, you are going to Hampton for at least a year." So I went there, kicking and screaming.

Shortly after I arrived I found black kids who weren't so different, who also grew up in a multicultural environment and had similar experiences. I also learned a newfound respect for black people as I learned our history and how much we have to be proud of — something I never learned in high school. My family was a part of black history in my community and in my state, and I knew to be proud of them, but I didn't know how proud I could be and should be of being black.

You always measure a man by how far he comes, not just by where he is. We came from being property to sitting with presidents. That is a long way for a people to come in a hundred years. That school year completely balanced my life.

After the end of the first year my mom called. "Well," she said, "do you want to transfer or not? It's up to you."

"No," I said. "I think I'm going to stay."

For the first time I felt as though I fit into a black community, and I didn't want to give it up and start over. That summer I came home with a haircut, a high-top fade. I walked through the door with this haircut, and with a look of horror my mother said, "I wanted you to become black, but not that black."

Several years later, my mother and I were walking back from the annual dinner for the graduating students and their parents. I knew the graduation list had been posted, and I wanted to share the results with my mother.

"Mom, there's something I need to tell you about graduation," I said, and a look of fear came over her face. We stopped and she leaned against a car and looked at me with great anticipation. "What?" she asked, with a look that said Oh God, what is he going to tell me now. Then I told her, "Mom, I'm number one in my class. I'm the valedictorian."

My mother burst into tears. She realized I had succeeded and so had she. Going to a black college was probably the best maturing experience in my life, because it taught me how to move in a black environment with the same ease as I had been able to move in a white one. I owe it all to my mother.

Sacred Bond

KEITH CLINKSCALES & MARGARET ANN CLINKSCALES

Some people seem to think that unless a black man has grown up urban and poor he hasn't had the

authentic black experience. Several of the men I interviewed grew up in middle-class suburban communities and remembered being called "Oreo," "white boy," or "Uncle Tom" by their black peers in other neighborhoods. With his mother's help, Keith Clinkscales was able to successfully avoid that kind of alienation. ■ A 1988 Connecticut Teacher of the Year, Margaret Ann Clinkscales currently teaches in the Bridgeport public school system. His father, Alvin Clinkscales, a former Harlem Globetrotter, is now a college administrator. Together they provided a comfortable life for their family, and his mother made a special effort to make sure Clinkscales felt at home not only in their white, middle-class community but also in a predominantly black one. His ability to move in these two worlds with ease and understanding eventually proved an integral part of his success. As founder of the magazine *Urban Profiles,* and now as president of *Vibe* – one of the hottest urban hip-hop music magazines in the country – Clinkscales has made a career of bringing the stories and images of the urban black experience to the rest of the world. ■ His mother understood the issues her children faced growing up black and middle-class. She also understood the need for them to be exposed to the diversity within the black community. Clinkscales is "authentic" by anyone's standards – largely the result of his mother's influence.

KEITH CLINKSCALES
President/CEO, Vibe *Magazine*
AGE THIRTY-FOUR
MOTHER MARGARET ANN CLINKSCALES

———

My brother, sister, and I grew up in a very suburban town in Connecticut. My family was fortunate because my mother and father both did well in their careers, but my mom made sure that I never felt or believed that I was above the brothers who lived in the projects down the street. It was really important to my mother that we were grounded. I think in her travels and in her circles, certainly in my father's circles, she had seen black men and women and their children who had grown out of touch with certain things. My mother was firmly against Jack and Jill [a national family organization founded to enrich the lives of black children. Membership consists primarily of middle-class families]. She thought it was elitist, so she just wasn't going for it. All of my friends went, and it turns out my wife is a child of Jack and Jill. But my mother was never one down to go to all the little black suburban society events.

We were middle class, not upper-middle class. I'm not saying that to give the impression that things were at all rough, because they weren't. There was nothing that I wanted. I can't remember being deprived of anything. I never went to bed hungry. I can never even remember the discussion of money being tight coming up in the household. But at the same time, we were not so rich that we could be out of touch with the world.

I think my mother knew that too. A lot of my family lived in the city; my mother's sister and my cousins all lived in Bridgeport. It served as a reminder: don't ever think you're better than anybody, because you ain't that far removed. My parents, especially my mom, rarely if ever spoke down on people. Even when black people were doing wrong, she took a lot of time to make sure I had a positive perception of black people to counter anything negative we may have seen. I think that racial pride helped me negotiate a very serious situation, being the only black kid in my schools.

The thing about growing up in an all white neighborhood is that it didn't matter if you were fair skinned, or even one-nineteenth black, black is black and you were a nigger to them. I often faced racism just by going to school, the basic kid-racism, not the advanced high-tech racism. I've been tied to a telephone pole, had black chalk put on my face, and got into a lot of fights. I experienced the blunt-edged meanness of children, and my mom helped me deal with that. Once I got in a really bad fight at school. When I came home my mother asked me why I got into a fight. I told her that a kid called me a nigger. She rarely condoned fighting, but this time it was like, "okay, whatever you did was justified." She supported me. And when the school called, she told them to make sure this never happens again. My mother ain't to be played with. So she stood by me in that particular instance. She had enough faith in me as her son to know I wouldn't use the excuse that someone called me a nigger every time I got in trouble. That has always meant something to me.

It was hard to outsmart my mom, because she knew something about everything. She knew something about the pick-and-roll; she knew something about rap music; she knew something about whatever was important to us, from cartoons to GI Joe dolls. She knew because she was forever reading. And she expected a high level of performance from me. As long as I can remember bringing home a report card, a C was unacceptable. If I brought home a D, I could get shot. She said that the only C she wanted to see on my report was the one in Clinkscales. I never brought home a C until high school. I thought it was going to be the end of the world. But by that time, my mother knew it wasn't my normal way of rolling and that I was working hard. She was always supportive in whatever I did.

I remember when I came out of Harvard and launched *Urban Profiles,* I had just finished spending the money I had borrowed from my parents to get through business school. They put me through college; I had a scholarship, but they paid all my incidental expenses and hanging-out money, so they were probably several thousand deep on college. And after I got my MBA, I wasn't talking about taking one of these big-money jobs. I told my mom I was going to continue to do my magazine. They didn't even question my decision. And though I never relied on it, I knew if I screwed up completely I could always move home. So the first year out when I was doing that magazine, I made $14,000. Now that was self-imposed poverty, but I'm going to tell you something, self-imposed poverty has its own drama. Because you're always thinking, why am I doing this to myself? I can go call so-and-so tomorrow and get a job, get a check, and be out of this. But I knew if I didn't find a way to build a business from the ground up, I would never have that skill.

My father did a good job of explaining racism to me, because he played for the Globetrotters. He told me stories of racism that were shocking to me. The team would play in some of the best places in the world and couldn't stay in the hotels. My father told me a story about going down to Washington, D.C., with the team. They went to this fancy restaurant after they had been rejected by three others. The restaurant manager said, oh sure, we'll seat you. So they sat down, and as soon as the team started to eat their meal the restaurant people put these screens up around them so the other patrons couldn't see them. Through his stories, I had a good sense of what racism was.

Both my father and my mother grew up kind of tough. My mother lived in Bridgeport with her sister and her uncle. They were not wealthy. They lived in a two-bedroom place and had to work hard to make it. My father was an orphan. He and his three brothers were brought up to Bridgeport from South Carolina, and lived in a house with twenty-five other young men. In the face of my parents' legacy, it would be wrong to come off like I grew up hard. I didn't. I grew up fortunate, but a smart person learns from the experience of others. I grew up the way I wish all black families could. But at the same time, I don't give a damn how much money you have, if you are born black, there are still traps out there that you have to be aware of. And you have to be equipped, because sometimes the smarter and more successful you are, the bigger target you become.

My mother was fortunate in that she was raising her children where she didn't have to fear for our lives. Of course anything can happen to anybody, anywhere, but I wasn't in a situation like my friends in the hood where every day even walking to school something could happen. My mother had to worry about the same things my friends' mothers did when I was hanging out with them, and she taught me to realize the potential dangers of hanging out there, even though she didn't want me to look down on the ghetto. But on a day-to-day basis, my mother had a different set of concerns — in many ways just as tough. She had to deal with all of the issues facing suburban kids, like access to drugs, fast cars, parties, and having the money to do what we wanted to do. She also had to deal with the issues of us being black and middle-class. Those are hard things for a mother to deal with, and my mom rose to the occasion.

RICHARD SPEARS & JANET SPEARS

The issue of identity can be especially complicated for biracial children. Among other complex

circumstances, some of them are often confused about which side of their dual heritage to adopt as their

own – but not Richard Spears. Although his white mother has been the primary influence in his life, he

is more definitive about his racial identity than the other biracial men I interviewed. He identifies with

African American culture almost exclusively, so I raised the question How does a white woman raise a

son with such a strong sense of identity as a black man? Spears's answer is simple: You have to meet my

mother. ■ To hear Janet Spears speak, there is no doubt that she has spent a lot of time in the hood.

And seeing them together, it's obvious why Spears calls her his hero. Most of the goals he has set for

himself and achieved – from building a business, to getting involved with his community, to raising a

loving family – have been inspired by his mother. The president of his own real estate company, Spears

is also president of 100 Black Men of New Jersey and the New Jersey Association of Black

Realtors. ■ Spears and his mother have had their share of struggles, but he knew that in order to be

completely at ease with who he is, he had to accept his white mother. The success of their relationship is

a tribute to the power of the mother-son bond to transcend race, and their story confirms that yes, a

strong white woman can indeed raise a strong black man.

RICHARD SPEARS
Real Estate Broker
AGE THIRTY-FIVE
MOTHER JANET SPEARS

I am the product of a mixed marriage of the sixties. My father was born in Corinth, Mississippi, and is black, black as shoe polish. So there ain't no doubt he is black. My mother is white. Her grandparents were from Poland and did not speak English when they came to this country. When she decided to get with my father, my grandfather decided he didn't have a daughter anymore. For years there were family members I didn't even know on the white side. Eventually my grandmother divorced my grandfather over this, because he made her choose between him and her daughter. She chose her daughter.

It was not just the white part of the family my mother had problems with. Every two or three years we would go to Mississippi to visit my grandmother on my father's side. The last time I went there, when I was maybe eleven, I remember sitting at the breakfast table having a typical southern breakfast, and I can remember the plate going around and my grandmother serving my brother and me, serving my father and his brothers, and skipping my mother. And it kept going and it kept skipping. And it didn't dawn on me that my father's mother hated my mother. At one point she referred to my mother as the white ghost, which is why, needless to say, we never went back there. My mother, being who she is, couldn't bite her tongue, and words were said. So she got it from both sides.

I can't hate white people, even though there is still a lot of racism that goes on in the world. To hate white people is to hate myself. I may be half-and-half, but I ain't never checked off "white" on an application. I've always been proud being African American, even though I really had more white people raising me than black people. I hear a lot of people who are mixed say that they're this and they're that, and I'm sorry, I'm a firm believer that if you've got some black in you, you're black. That's how the outside world looks at you. You can be whatever you want to yourself, but you're still black to the rest of the world.

My mom is real. And how "real" she was used to embarrass me. Society says you should be a certain way, especially when you first meet people, but my mother never puts on airs. She is loud and boisterous. You either love her or hate her. My mother is a college-educated woman, but she probably had more street friends than she had educated friends. I don't think she could name three people with whom she went to college, whereas she could name everyone on that street corner; and I mean, my mom was a hustler. Point blank. My mom traded food stamps. People would come with food stamps, and she'd give them money. But it wasn't dollar for dollar, trust me on that. The alcoholics came with their food stamps, and she knew that they were going to buy booze, and she'd make sure first that they had taken care of their family and that they had food for themselves, and then she'd cut the deal.

One thing I think is real important to understand is that I had an African American father who wanted to be white and a Caucasian mother who thought she was black. My mother will use the word "nigger" in a room full of black people and no one in the room will turn around. It's like when black folks use it with each other, for some reason it doesn't have the same effect. Like when you see your boy and say, "What's up, nigger, how you doing?" It's almost a loving term.

I always knew my mother was white, but I guess when it really came to a head was in the sixth grade. I had just gone to a new elementary school and I was doing well. I can remember my mother was big on us bringing our papers home and showing them to her. I remember getting report cards with straight A's, but then I got a B in a class. "Let me see that," my mother said. "How could you get a B? I got all your papers."

"I don't know, Ma," I told her. "I never got less than a 90."

My mother went to talk to the teacher to find out why. I think, first of all, she was surprised my mother was white. The woman tried to claim that anything between 90 and 92 was a B in her class. Well, my mother said, "I'd like to see your grade book for the rest of the class." And she saw that my teacher had given other students with a 90 average an A-minus or an A.

"Change the grade," my mother said.

"I don't see why it's important," the teacher said. "What difference does it make, he's still in the Honor Society."

"You white bitch," my mother yelled, and lifted the desk up and dumped it on the teacher. No one messed with her baby and got away with it. Right then and there I thought, I guess you are white, but you're just a trip. To my mom's credit, she wouldn't take shit from anybody.

My mother and father started buying houses in our neighborhood, little two-family houses. We had five rental properties,

all of them on our block. My brothers and I would cut the grass, shovel the sidewalks, and collect the rent. We didn't come from a family that believed in allowances and stuff like that. That was just part of your job. You got a roof over your head, you had clothes on your back. We never knew we had money. We were lower-middle class who became middle class, but we never knew we got there until we grew up. I now think that was good, because it kept me grounded.

My parents stayed married for eighteen years. When I left for college they got divorced – over another woman, from what I understood later. My father drove away and never came back. My mother thought love was forever; everything was in his name. So when the divorce went through he gave her nothing. Not the house that we were living in, none of the rental properties, although she was the one who built it all up. My mother just couldn't deal with it. She had worked her whole life to get to this point, and now she was worse off than when she started. My mother shut down. She eventually had a nervous breakdown.

It was during this time, probably the only time our lives, that my mother and I butted heads. I had a car my senior year of high school, and I worked two jobs. I then got accepted to college and you couldn't tell me nothing. One time I told my mother I was going to a party. I told her I would be back at midnight, but got home at 1:30 a.m. So with all of the stuff brewing in her mind she started yelling and screaming at me. She said the one thing that hurt me more than anything else she could have ever said: "You're going to be just like your father...." She could have stabbed me, she could have beaten me, and it wouldn't have hurt as much as that. Maybe she realized that she had said the wrong thing, but she didn't know how to take it back. So we just coexisted for the next month and a half, before I graduated. I woke up, I did my chores, but we didn't speak.

It wasn't until I was driving up to Syracuse, on my way to college, that things changed. My father had let me down again; he was supposed to drive me up there. So we're driving up, and it is a real quiet trip, no one saying anything. Then my mother sees a sign, "Syracuse, sixty miles." And she just starts crying, she's just laid out. I knew why she was crying, but I didn't say anything. She told me she was sorry. "It's all right, Ma," I told her. "I know what you are going through." Right then and there our relationship changed.

I think, though, in college was the only time I felt embarrassed that my mother was white. There would be a parents' weekend each year, and my freshman year I asked her not to come. I had already integrated myself at school, and even though Syracuse University was only 10 percent black, to me, coming from an all-white high school, it was like mecca. I had hit pay dirt. I had a black girlfriend, black friends. I pledged a black fraternity, and everything for me was black, black, black. I wasn't even speaking to white people, other than my roommates. Hardly anyone knew my mother was white. I just didn't feel it was necessary to talk about it.

At some point later in my freshman year, my mother sprung back from her breakdown, and she said, "Everything I had I will have again." By my sophomore year, she had snapped out of her depression. I asked her to come to parents' weekend and she came. My fraternity brothers couldn't believe this woman. She just came in being rowdy. "MF this; You bastards better get yourselves together; Who's that pretty girl? Well, an ugly thing like you shouldn't even be with her." I mean, she was crackin' hard, and my frat brothers thought she was a trip. They all loved her. My mother always embraced my friends. She figures if they're my friends, then they're her friends.

Just before I left for college my mother asked me to promise her one thing: "Don't fall in love with a white woman." I think she was saying she didn't want me to go through what she did. So, obviously, it had had an effect on her. But you know, I am really proud of my mom. She was the doting mother and a career woman before it was even fashionable. She was working two jobs, and I can remember that all through Little League baseball she never missed a game. Those are the things you remember. Those are the things that count. She was always there for my brothers and me. And now she is a permanent part of the scenery in my life and in the lives of my children.

She is my hero. To have gone through what she went through: losing her family, going through a divorce, having a

nervous breakdown, losing all of her property, and to come back on top – she's a remarkable woman. I'm sure she wishes she could have skipped some of the pain, but I think all of her trials and tribulations made my mother a tougher person. I still hold my breath when I go into new situations with her. I am still working on her mouth, but I'm not embarrassed anymore. This is my mother, this is who she is. She is real.

TAKASHI NORRIS & MOTOKO NORRIS

BALANCE AND HARMONY

The son of an African American father, Dr. James Norris, and a Japanese mother, Motoko Norris, Takashi Norris is unique among the biracial men I spoke to. Unwilling to define himself by race, he gladly embraces both of his parents' wildly different cultures. Norris believes that to do any differently would be to deny one of the two people he values most in life. As a result, he is as comfortable with his father's large extended family in the Tidewater area of Virginia as he is with his mother's traditional close-knit family in Tokyo. ▪ His intimate understanding of these two societies gives him an edge in his job at the American Chamber of Commerce in Tokyo, which promotes commerce and trade between the U.S. and Japan. As the special assistant for External Affairs, he is instrumental in building relationships with Japanese industries and government agencies for the Chamber. Having built bridges between the two distinct branches of his family, encouraging relationships in business comes naturally. ▪ When I met Norris he had a few points about his mother written down so he wouldn't forget them. He particularly wanted to mention the impact of his mother's sense of independence and individuality, which helped him successfully integrate his two cultures into a unique personal identity. This mother-son relationship resulted in a man who lives free of racial stereotypes and the pressures associated with being biracial in America.

TAKASHI NORRIS
Administrator,
American Chamber of Commerce, Japan
AGE TWENTY-NINE
MOTHER MOTOKO NORRIS

My mother never felt comfortable with me calling her Mother or Mom, so I call her by her name, Motoko. My mother was twenty-one when she had me, and I've always felt she was not only a mother, but like an older sister, too. Many people have said that we look like brother and sister, because at twenty-nine my mother probably looked around twenty-two. In a sense, as I was growing up, my mother was growing up too.

My parents met when my father was attending a doctor's meeting in Tokyo. My mother was nineteen, my father thirty-three. She was working in a pearl shop and had a strong interest in learning English, so she took care of a lot of foreign customers. She sold my father pearls. He says he fell in love with her when he first saw her. My mother says for her their meeting was more or less another chance to speak English. It's a bone of contention with them.

They got married in the States, and my mother did not tell her parents about it right away. At that time, a lot of the information her parents received about blacks came from other foreigners who told them to beware of black people. After my mother told her parents about the marriage, her father didn't speak to her for six months. Her mother said that she was going to be "cheated" because my father is a black man. My grand-mother on my father's side said, "James, why couldn't you marry a colored girl?" Those were her words. I don't think she was happy either, but both my mother and my father came from very loving families, so it just took a little bit of time.

Now there's a strong bond between the families. My mother's parents have visited my father's mother and family in Virginia. One of my father's sisters went to Japan and stayed with my grandparents. When my mother's mother passed away, my father's family sent letters of condolences, flowers, and money. I think it takes effort. You have to put in some time, and if you're patient enough and loving enough, the end result will always be good.

My mother always felt comfortable with my father's family. I think her sense of individuality, her sense of adventure, and her sense of exploration helped.

When she was seventeen, before she met my father, she went abroad and stayed with a family in Portland, Oregon, for a year to study English. This was in the early sixties, and during that time it was still unheard-of for a young Japanese woman to travel thousands of miles away and stay in a foreign land, especially without a strong knowledge of the language and the culture. Her father didn't agree with her decision, but my mother was determined to go.

I think that my mother's strong sense of individuality carried on to me. My mother told me, "You don't have to be a stereotype, just distinguish yourself. It doesn't make a difference if you are African American or Japanese, first and foremost understand who you are." That's what she taught me. For me, race is not a determining factor of a person's character or personality; culture is. No one has ever forced me to choose a side. When there was a box to be checked to identify my race, I always checked "other." What my parents did was expose me at an early age to both my cultures. Beginning when I was a year old, I would spend two or three months in Japan every summer, completely immersed in the culture with my Japanese relatives. During school breaks, we would go down to Virginia, and I would be immersed in the culture of my African American relatives.

My parents did that on purpose. They knew I should be exposed to both cultures and integrate them into who I am. And at times, I have to know how to separate them, too. If I were to go to Virginia and start bowing to the people down there, they're not going to understand what I'm doing. When I see my relatives in Japan, I bow automatically. That is an instinctive thing that you just learn over time. You say thank you and kind of put your head down. But in Virginia, everybody gives hugs and kisses. It is something we do. We're always holding each other and saying, "I love you." That is not done in Japan. I remember when one of my Japanese cousins got married. She was with her husband in front of about fifty people, and I went up to kiss her. She got frightened. I said I was sorry, that I had forgotten. There are times I have to be careful, because in Japanese culture you have to act a certain way at a certain time. I think my black side is a lot more open. There's a clear difference between the two.

When I was growing up, during my time in Japan I was teased. Out of the one hundred Japanese kids in the nursery school I attended for a while, I was different. They didn't really know what I was, so rather than categorizing me as black or white, they just called me "gaijin," which means foreigner. The Japanese have a prejudice against foreigners,

not against a background or color, it's just if you're not Japanese. I felt I was able to overcome that because of my mother. She would tell me, "You have to feel that you're important. You're human, and don't ignore it. Even though you're not Japanese, you are Takashi." I think if you're different and you feel negative about your difference, people will feel that. I was able to turn their prejudice around in many ways. When I was twelve, rather than be afraid I opened myself up to them, and I taught kids how to speak English. As soon as they understood that I wanted to show them my difference, but at the same time I was human just like they were, everything was okay.

One thing my mother always said to me is you will be judged by your appearance. You have to pay attention to every detail. She loses all respect for a man who's impeccably dressed and well groomed but has dirty shoes or dirty fingernails. I do my best to look good for certain functions if I am with my mother, even though I feel very comfortable with jeans and a T-shirt. That's my style. She never forced me to dress, but she gave me a lot of advice. She would say, "If you want to be one step ahead of the next person, you should pay attention to details, because people do." I think females do tend to pay more attention to detail than males do, and I got that from her. I think she instilled in me a little bit of her female character.

Even though my mother was a stickler about appearance, she always placed the mind as the most important thing in a person. When I was about thirteen, I remember posing in front of the mirror. I was a skinny kid and was always conscious about my thin body, so I'd really work out and I'd pose in front of the mirror. My mother laughed. "What are you doing that for?" she said. "You can look good, but it's what's up here in the head that's going to make the difference."

My mother has been a very strong presence in my life. Even if she's thousands of miles away, I feel she's thinking about me. But even more than that, she has been a great influence in me developing a strong sense of character, a sense of self worth, and a sense of identity as a person, as a human being, as Takashi.

59

JONAH MARTIN EDELMAN & MARIAN WRIGHT EDELMAN

MAMA'S BOY

Jonah Martin Edelman was also born into a family with two strong cultural traditions – one African American, one Jewish. But neither race nor class has been as influential to his life as the political identity of his mother, Marian Wright Edelman, founder of the Children's Defense Fund. Like so many men with prominent mothers, he has had a tremendous example to follow. Edelman is making his own way, but he is doing so by building on his mother's legacy of service. As executive director of Stand for Children, an affiliate of the Children's Defense Fund, he works to create grassroots support systems for children across the country. ■ His parents met while doing civil rights work in Mississippi; his mother was a lawyer for the NAACP Legal Defense Fund, and his father was an aide for the late U.S. senator Robert Kennedy. In 1968 they became the first interracial couple married in the State of Virginia after the U.S. Supreme Court legalized interracial marriage. Their marriage has lasted thirty years and has produced three sons. ■ Edelman's mother is a powerful woman and a relentless advocate for children in this country. Even while they were being photographed, she and her son were debating the work that needed to be done. Although their personal relationship has evolved into a professional one, the trust and admiration they've shared remain constant. In her son, Marian Wright Edelman has an heir to her legacy of service. In his mother, Edelman has found a sense of purpose, and a better understanding of who he is.

JONAH MARTIN EDELMAN
Executive Director, Stand for Children
AGE TWENTY-SEVEN
MOTHER MARIAN WRIGHT EDELMAN

I was a mama's boy. I only wanted to go places with my mom. The first thing she did whenever we met somebody new, famous or not, was say, "Have you met my son?" You really feel like you're somebody when the first thing your parents do is introduce you. They were always thinking, who can you meet or who should you talk to so you can learn and develop? So from very early on I remember meeting lots of interesting people because my parents made a point of it.

In political circles, my mother and father are both part of the liberal establishment. But the funny thing is that my mother is deeply conservative. Anyone who says that she is liberal doesn't really know her, they know certain policy positions held by the Children's Defense Fund. When I was growing up, she was more strict than my dad, and always the most strict of any of my friends' parents. That was frustrating, but it was a great, grounding force for me.

Even though they were both extremely busy people, both my mother and father were very involved in our upbringing. But my mom took on the more traditional mother role. She expected it of herself. My mom would get up in the morning and make us breakfast. Now that I have a demanding job myself, to think that she got up every single day and made us breakfast was remarkable. She was traveling quite a bit, often two or three times a week. I always remember my mother being there at significant moments though, the PTA meetings, the parent/teacher nights, and the Little League games. I can remember her reading to us all the time, the Greek myths, fairy tales, Bible stories, and African folk tales. She was the proto-typical supermom in that era when the mother basically did everything. And that takes a toll. Looking back, I realize that my mother was able to do it by not sleeping. She would sleep maybe three to five hours a night for years. Knowing the history of her organization, with all the fund-raising and all the programs, it's incredible how she was able to balance family and work. But I never felt jealousy or that I was competing with our mother's work. She missed only one of my birthdays. She was on some kind of presidential delegation in South Africa and she still feels guilty about it! So I don't have any pain associated with that, because it wasn't the pattern. I always felt special, and I always felt like my brothers and I were the most important things in my mother's life.

My mother is from a long line of Baptist ministers in the South. She grew up with the church being central in her existence. My father's Jewish. Religion played a bigger role and was a larger gulf than race in my parents' relationship. It was very important to my mother that we grew up with religious grounding, yet she knew full well that a mixed marriage, racially and religiously, meant that there were compromises to be made. They were always trying to strike a balance; my brothers and I all had bar mitzvah ceremonies. We did it in our backyard, not a synagogue. My mother's side of the family was heavily involved in the service; hymns were sung; yet we had a rabbi and did the chanting of the Torah. It was really an interesting mixture of traditions. But because my mother was always much more religious than my father – though actually at this point he's becoming more religious – the tides pulled me towards Christianity, despite the great respect that I have for Judaism.

My sense of being biracial might be different from a lot of people's. When I was growing up it wasn't so common. Most people think I am Latino, either Puerto Rican or Dominican. There weren't yet these debates about a mixed-race category. I think the way our history dictates, if you are one drop black, then you are considered black. But it's obviously much more complicated when you're growing up. I think your racial con-

sciousness is a function of where you live, what you're taught by your parents, and then, fundamentally, what you look like. That dictates how the world perceives you and how you are treated.

Prior to college I had a sense that I understood both races well. But the reality was that I understood the white side of myself better, because that was what I had known. And it was only in college that I went on a journey to understand my black heritage, appreciate it, and draw strength from it. My mother was instrumental in that. She had a real desire to be there and talk to me about these issues, not with impatience but with understanding. I remember one conversation in particular we had in New Haven when I was a freshman at Yale. She was really happy that I had begun dealing with these identity issues. And in this conversation she explained a lot about her life. What made this special was that my mother is not someone who talks about herself. Not at all. She listens incredibly well. If you're

63

in a conversation with her, at the end of it sometimes you'll realize that she hasn't said anything, but you think it's been a great conversation. She's very much future-and-present oriented. It is rare that she'll reminisce about things. But this time she opened up to me. She talked about her upbringing in the South, her experiences as a lawyer, things that happened in Mississippi during the civil rights movement, and why she formed the Children's Defense Fund. She told me stories I had never heard before, like how she learned how to fly a plane in Mississippi because she was one of very few lawyers there and needed to get around the state quickly. This is somebody who is very afraid of heights. She blew me away. She told me the stories of going to different jailhouses and looking at young men who had gotten beaten up by the police. She told me about defending them and dealing with some of the sheriffs down there.

That summer, my mother and I went driving through the South, starting in Atlanta and traveling through to the Mississippi Delta to see the giants of the civil rights movement. The trip was for my benefit more than anything else. Going to the Delta was a profound experience for me. It showed me a period in history that you read about in textbooks. Being down there, meeting and talking to those people, brought home the reality of it, the risks and the fears that people actually experienced as they tried to make social change. Afterwards I definitely understood my mother better, as well as myself.

My mother has been a powerful figure in my life; just look at what I'm doing now. I'm running this affiliate to her organization. We're still striking a balance between the professional and the personal in our relationship, and I think that it's been good. I've learned a lot more about her and she's learned a lot more about me. We don't agree all the time, and I think some-times she wished I had less of an opinion. Obviously there is a fundamental respect, but she is the boss. She is unbelievably effective. She has relentless drive and is very demanding. She knows what's right and she doesn't doubt it. Growing up with her work ethic has helped me.

I do think mothers raising black sons have a special burden. They have the responsibility of giving their kids the armor to deal with a world that assumes the worst of them, of helping their sons go through life without being beaten down by all the bad looks or the assumptions. And my mother did that for me and my brothers; she gave us the armor, despite the circumstance of our privileged upbringing and being mixed. She's always saying, "You're black, and this is something you should be proud of no matter what anyone says. You have a rich heritage on both sides and you should be proud of that." She was very conscious of imbuing us with the notion that we are who we are, that we are special, and basically no other opinion matters. The struggle is harder for a mother who is raising her children in the hood, but I think the challenge is similar.

My mother always had very high expectations for us, but she always made us feel like we were loved unconditionally, so if I stumble, the love is still there. It's not contingent. I never had to worry about that. I always knew my parents were proud of me when I did something good, but they would have been proud of me and loved me no matter what. Even if I were to become an investment banker and my sole interest in life was to make a lot of money, she'd love me anyway. But you can bet that my mother would be hitting me up for contributions.

Sacred Bond

ERNEST DREW JARVIS & CHARLENE DREW JARVIS

Family plays a major role in defining who we are, no matter how hard we try to distinguish ourselves as separate entities. I interviewed a number of men from accomplished families with prominent mothers at the helm, and for better or worse, their family names carried weight. Among these men, Ernest Drew Jarvis seemed to feel the pressure of that weight more than most. Although Jarvis jokingly tried to dismiss the significance of being the son of Charlene Drew Jarvis, it is a subtle yet constant presence in his life — even in areas in which he'd rather it wasn't, like his romantic life. ■ A former scientist with the National Institutes of Health, his mother is now a member of the Washington, D.C., city council and president of Southeast University, a new college in the District. Unwilling to compete with his family's legacy, Jarvis is trying to do things his own way. In addition to brokering commercial real estate deals, Jarvis is founder of Metropolitan Access, a networking organization that presents noted speakers from government and business to African American professionals. Part of his motivation to establish the group was his mother's philosophy that there is more to life than just making money. ■ Jarvis's relationship with his mother has given him access to people and information, but in the end he says it's the private side that is most important. Their relationship is an example of how integrally our sense of identity is linked to our family, especially to our mothers.

ERNEST DREW JARVIS
Commercial Real Estate
AGE THIRTY-FIVE
MOTHER CHARLENE DREW JARVIS

On my mother's side I am a fourth-generation Washingtonian, and a fifth-generation Washingtonian on my father's side. My father's family were undertakers. They started their business in 1902, and it grew to be the largest black-owned funeral home on the East Coast. My mother's father was Dr. Charles Drew, the black scientist who discovered a way to store blood plasma. That was during World War II, when there was no method of preserving blood to get it to injured soldiers on the battlefield. My grandfather found a way to do it, and it has saved millions of lives since. Probably up until 1960, there weren't many black surgeons who weren't trained by him.

As the story goes, he died because white hospital workers refused to give him a blood transfusion after an automobile accident in North Carolina. But that's not what really happened. The story was changed by the civil rights folks who used my grandfather as a kind of poster boy. He was actually going from Washington to Atlanta to make a speech, after having just performed a twelve-hour surgery. He was exhausted and fell asleep behind the wheel. He did get into an accident, but we understand he did get good treatment. The three black physicians who treated him said he wouldn't have been able to survive, and if he had, he would have been a vegetable. He was beyond help. The other story is great PR, but it's not the truth.

What Dr. Charles Drew did for both myself and my mother was to create a legacy that has always been a part of our lives. My mother was only seven years old when he died in 1950. Even though he wasn't around for most of it, she had this great looming figure in her life. She was always "the daughter of Charles Drew," and there was a certain level of expectation that went with it. Of his children, my mom was the one who inherited his drive. She's the one who just moves forward and who is both physically and intellectually imposing. She is a large woman, six feet tall and broad shouldered. She received a Ph.D. in neuropsychology and worked at the National Institutes of Health, one of the first black scientists at NIH who studied the brain.

But when I was growing up, my mother had two lives; she studied the brain all day, and when she came home she was a traditional wife and mother. When I turned sixteen, she said, enough of that. She just walked away from NIH and became engaged in the politics of the city. In 1979, she put all of her efforts into the city council race and won. She's still a council member. She has had a couple of close races, but she is virtually unbeatable. I think the person who had to make the biggest adjustment to my mother's new life was my father, because he was a traditionalist — it was his house and he made the dough. When they went out together he was introduced as "Ernie Jarvis, Charlene's husband." For a brother who thinks of his wife as a homemaker, that didn't go over well. Eventually my father said, enough. He couldn't handle being "the husband of." They divorced my second year of college, and my mother immersed herself in her work. Because my mother was single, I got a lot of opportunities to go to black tie events with her. I got to meet presidents, I got to meet Jesse Jackson, and I got to meet Louis Farrakhan. I got hooked on it. I would go behind the dais and behind the curtains where the VIPs and the elected officials were. I found all that intriguing, but I never really felt pressured to measure up to the legacy.

At that time I wasn't focused enough to meet the standards and expectations of my parents and grandparents. I had an idea about what I wanted to do with my life, but I never felt I had to succeed, because I knew that I'd fall short. I don't mind competing, but I knew I was not going to be Charles Drew or a scientist like my mom. To me, quite honestly, what the legacy meant was that I didn't wait in lines for registration. When I transferred from Morehouse to Howard, everybody there knew me because of my grandfather and my mother. Although my mother always encouraged me to do well, she never really said, these are the expectations I have of you, or, you have to handle yourself in a certain way. I grew up like any other normal middle-class kid with educated parents.

My mother was a typical mom but one with more energy than anyone else I have ever met. Her drive is unparalleled. When my mother ran for mayor in 1990, my brother, who was a year younger than me, and I got up at seven o'clock in the morning with her to pass out literature. She went straight out till midnight. My brother couldn't hang. He got tired and took the subway home and took a nap. I hung with her, but I was exhausted.

I was looking at her schedule one day and I said, damn, there's no way I could do this. She was up at five, and went to bed at two. Every day of the week for a year. I just said, damn, and here I am,

just chilling. I'm going to the beach and chasing skirts and hanging out with my boys. And she's doing all this. So that's the first time I really said, Ernie, you got to do something with your life. I always thought, you drive a Porsche, live in a big house in Bethesda, belong to a country club, buy a boat, and life's great, right? My mother says to me, "That's not it, son."

"Ernie," my mother says, "you're thirty-five now, it's time to stop running." Every Sunday morning when I go to her house she begins, "Ernie, I don't understand how come you're not married." I'm like, here we go. "Don't you want kids?"

"Well, right now I'm reading the paper, so just chill," I'll say, and I know that it's not over. Once when she pursued it and asked again, "Well, why don't you have kids?" I thought, here's my opportunity. "The reason I don't have kids is because everybody I dated was pro-choice," I said, and she just looked at me and said, "You're so disgusting," and took her cup of coffee and the paper and went upstairs. That was fine. I wanted her to leave me alone.

Another favorite topic is the car I drive. I drive a red 'Vette. I'm not the community servant like she is. I'm out to get mine, like the young'uns say. Recently she said, "You need a nice BMW or a Lexus now." She says I'm sending out the wrong message to the young ladies, that I'm a player. I told her that's exactly what I am. But I'm definitely getting tired of running. I look at my Visa bill, and the time I spent chasing women, and it's a lot.

I don't tend to introduce many women to my mother, because sisters are so focused on getting married, they take it the wrong way. Before turning thirty-two, I would drop by all the time with girlfriends or dates. But now if women are between thirty-two and thirty-five, they're going berserk. Regardless of what they do professionally, they are focused on getting a man. It's awkward if I don't think that way about them, because women

will interpret meeting my mother as sign of serious intent. So I try to shy away from it, but it's hard because my mother only lives about five minutes away from me. I still get mail there, so I run back and forth. It's almost like I have two houses. If there's somebody of some significance who I want to meet my mother, I'll say, Mama, drop by. I want you to meet so-and-so.

But my mother's very cool. She never says to me, oh, I don't like her. I remember one time though, she didn't like a girl-friend. She couched it in a discus-sion about my former girlfriend, Lisa. She said, "Do you think Lisa has a good reputation?"

"I think she has a great reputation," I said.

She said, "What do you think your guy friends would say about Lisa?"

I explained how I thought they would think she's great and all that. She went on to ask what people in general would think if I were to marry her.

"People would think that

she's a catch," I said. "She's a nice girl from a nice family."

Then she said, "What about Barbara?" (This is not her real name.)

"About Barbara?" I said. "I'm not really sure, what do you mean?"

"I don't know," she said, "what do you think people would say about her?"

"Well, I think people would say that she was pretty wild in college...." And then I said, "I can't believe you did that!" So instead of just saying, I don't think she's right for you, she sets me up. And in the end that was a very tactful way of saying, think about it.

I quite honestly believe there are some women who want to go out with me in order to say, "I date the son of Charlene Drew Jarvis." Washington's a fishbowl, and I think we all are intrigued by politicians' kids. Some of them are very obvious about it. I went out with a sister three or four weeks ago. She said, "How is your mom?" I said, "She's great, thanks for asking." I kind of sensed it was coming. The classic case of "it would be cool to hang out with the son of." Then she said, "Well, you-all pretty close?" "Yeah, she's my mother, why wouldn't we be?" And she stayed on it for about ten more minutes, and then I said, okay, I know what this is going to be. It's very apparent when they're trying to be slick about it.

I do think, however, "Are you and your mother close?" is a pretty standard question, irrespective of who my mother is. Women want to see if they married this guy, would his mother be at their house? Or will his mother be interfering in the relationship? They want to see if I'm a mama's boy.

When a girlfriend meets my mother, I can tell who is self-actualized and who is not. Some of the women I have gone out

with meet my mother and freak, like we're sitting at the breakfast table and they don't say anything but, pass the butter. And I'll ask, "How come you didn't say anything?"

"I didn't want to say anything stupid in front of your mother," they'll say. But I don't look at my mother like that, nor should she.

Then there are some women who go to the other extreme, and they'll say something like, "What do you think about the downfall of communism, Mrs. Jarvis?" My mother'll just look up and say, "I'm not sure about that." They are trying to impress her, like, I'm together, I'm on the ball. But they're not having breakfast with the public person, they're having breakfast with my mom. It's great to date people who walk in and say, "Hey, Charlene, what's up?" and never think about it. That's how I can gauge whether a person is comfortable with themselves, when they really don't give a damn about whose son I am.

WALTER WHITMAN & SHIRLEY WHITMAN

MOTHER  IS IN CONTROL

It is sometimes hard for our mothers to let us go, to let us venture out into the world and become our own men. I spoke with a number of men who said that there came a point in their relationship with their mother that they had to impose some distance in order to become close again. But Walter Whitman's mother never let her son get too far away — even when he wanted to. The closeness they shared wasn't something she was willing to relinquish without a fight. ■ From the moment his mother, Shirley Whitman, showed up at her son's choir rehearsal to be photographed for this book, her no-nonsense, charismatic presence commanded respect and attention from everyone. Her son is the founder, director, and patriarch of the Soul Children of Chicago, a popular youth choir that inspires audiences around the country and overseas. Over the last seventeen years, more than a thousand young people have sung with the choir. The alumni of Soul Children have gone on to a variety of professions, and many of them are now doctors, social workers, and even preachers. Whitman is as proud of them as his mother — the self-appointed matriarch of the choir — is of him. ■ His mother's presence in his life is stronger now than ever, and although their relationship is not always easy, Whitman realizes that not too many people enjoy the kind of devotion his mother lavishes on him. His greatest challenge in this relationship is to establish his own autonomy, but his greatest reward continues to be his mother's unconditional support.

WALTER WHITMAN
Choir Director, Soul Children of Chicago
AGE THIRTY-SIX
MOTHER SHIRLEY WHITMAN

I was twenty-one years old and my mother still didn't want me to move out of the house. I was saying, "Let me go!" She was saying, "No, you stay here, I'll fix you a little room." She wanted me there with her, and even now, fifteen years later, she still does. She wants an even closer relationship with me now that I've moved out. She gets upset if I go out of town and don't tell her, and if I tell her, she gets upset if I don't come by the house to see her before I leave. I find myself sometimes pulling away because she gets real intense, and sometimes it embarrasses me. She makes such a fuss when I'm around, and she's very protective of me and my brother.

When my mother retired, she felt she needed to do something more with her life, so the Soul Children became her project, and she has taken over. She has stepped in and dedicated herself to being my assistant. She has a great desire to help, and even though there are a lot of things she's still learning, Mother is in control. Everyone knows she is "Mother" and you don't say too much of anything around her. It's challenging. I'm working on trying to find a niche where she can do what she does best. She just pours herself into the choir; in a way, her work with it gives her a sense of self-worth. When my mother has a purpose, she is an intense, passionate, and very deliberate person.

Right now she's taking care of the finances of the organization. She wants everything done by the books and doesn't want anyone else to do it but her. She holds on to it. "Mother, please," I tell her, "Mrs. Johnson is my right and left hand, she won't let anything happen. She is very meticulous about the books." But my mother still comes in the office every day, and she'll count every shirt in the room, and she'll count every tape. My mother just wants to make sure everything is right. I once took a tape out of the box and gave it to somebody. My mother was running around, "There's a tape missing, there's a tape missing!"

"Calm down, Mother," I said. "I took the tape."

"Well, you need to let me know. I want to make sure...."

"It's not that serious, Mama," I said, but she's very passionate, and she's going to make sure that nothing happens to me, or the organization. She is a mother hen, and nobody can say anything about me. There is a side of my mother that will rise up and attack when it comes to her son: "Don't you be doing that to my son. What's wrong with you? Why you treating him like this?" She will defend me with a craziness.

The choir had a roast-and-toast for me, and let me tell you, my mother literally got upset, knowing the purpose of this event was to let me have it. It was hilarious. People were really dishing it out. I can't even remember what was being said, but they were calling me some names, and my mother jumped up.

"No! He ain't!" She went off.

"Ms. Whitman," they all tried to explain, "this is just a roast. No one is serious." Well, my mother just up and left, she was so upset. Everyone tried to stop her. "God, this is so embarrassing," I thought, but you can't help but love her. She is funny. Intense, but good. People have learned to understand that about her.

My mother is my number-one fan. She wants to go everywhere the choir goes. My father's the same way. They drove all the way from Chicago to Detroit to hear us sing, five hours up and five back. My mother makes sure all the family gets to the concerts. She makes sure everybody gets an invitation, she'll sell tickets, she'll beat 'em across the head if need be to make sure they're all there. My mother corrals people. When we have concerts, she has all of the relatives, sixty or seventy of them, sitting right there.

My mother gets such joy out of making a fuss over me. If I'm in a family situation it's like all eyes are on me. If I go to a family function, they all want to talk to me about Soul Children; I guess that could be a good thing, but for me it's a lot of pressure. I just want to be a family member, but the family wants to cater to me. The kids want to hang around, and the elders want to sit down and talk to me about the choir.

Our family is very close knit, and my mother is the one who helps keep it together. She keeps in contact with all the family, particularly her side. We were always together for Thanksgiving. Everybody knew my father would come four hours late to Thanksgiving dinners. Whenever he got there, the family always expected him to have a smile on his face. But he wasn't the main focus. It was always Shirley and the boys.

I'm not as connected to my relatives as I used to be. A lot of it is because I'm growing, and the family mind-set is not something I want to consistently be around — not in a negative way, but they don't really branch out too far. I'm one that branches out, but my mother keeps pulling me back

into the family. She won't let me stray too far. And besides, they are all very supportive of me.

No matter what I do, how I act, my mother just loves me, even after I've been downright mean. She can get beyond my faults, my shortcomings, and sometimes just my downright nasty behavior and still love me. I see it more now. Sometimes when my mother really gets on my last nerve, I'll try to see if I can make her mad enough to say, "Well, I'm not going to work for you no more!" I know it is a terrible way out, and it never works anyway. She doesn't budge. She's there, doing whatever she can do for me. If I need her for anything, she's there. She never says, "I ain't gonna do nothing for you, you don't deserve it!" I guess I have put up some barriers with my family, but even with those barriers, the family would say, "We're gonna break him down." They don't let me get away. They wouldn't let that happen, and my mother represents that unconditional love of the family. She represents wholeness for me. I know there's a side of me that has to be more grateful, because a lot of people don't have family like I have; they don't have a mother who will be there whenever you need her. I couldn't ask for more.

HERBIE QUINONES & ANA AYALA

JUST ME AND MY MOMS

Not all mothers are as demonstrative as Walter Whitman's mother. Some mothers are just more reserved about expressing affection toward their sons. Herbie Quinones was one of many who had to search for signs of his mother's feelings for him. He was part of a surprising percentage of men who said their mother "just wasn't the touchy-feely type" or "never came out and said 'I love you.'" But, like these other men, Quinones still knew that he was loved — he just had to work harder than most to find evidence of it. ▪ Ana Ayala is a small woman with a forbidding presence. In fact, this photograph captures one of the few times she cracked a smile while we were with her. Quinones grew up trying to get his mother to smile and trying to make others feel comfortable around her. He eventually turned comedy into a career. He produces educational videos for an AIDS outreach program by day, but by night and on weekends he hits the national comedy circuit doing stand-up. ▪ Despite his descriptions of dire punishments, Quinones broke down just thinking about what his mother has meant to his life and the sacrifices she has made for him. He has worked hard to understand his mother and her life, and with that understanding discovered she truly loves him and is proud of the man he has become. In the end this interview reveals how powerful the mother-son bond can be, even when the most important words are left unsaid.

HERBIE QUINONES
Comedian/AIDS Educator
AGE THIRTY-EIGHT
MOTHER ANA AYALA

———

My moms can carry a grudge like you wouldn't believe. She didn't speak to me for two years when I grew dreadlocks. Two years! She thought I had betrayed the Puerto Rican people and had rejected who I was. It's funny, because for me growing locks was the exact opposite. Being a dark-skinned Puerto Rican, I was embracing our African ancestry, something that we don't highlight often in Puerto Rican culture. The locks were also a way of expressing my pride in our Indian heritage. My moms didn't see it that way. She just saw her little boy stop combing his hair, and some old nappy shit growing out of it. So I have to give my moms some latitude. She had no point of reference. She still hasn't come around, but now she's talking to me at least.

Moms is stern, but she also can be warm once you get into her good graces. You can have her heart. So if you can deal with the psychosis and get to the good stuff, you'd find a heart of gold. It's just that my mother, she's not very open about her feelings, particularly towards me. She wasn't raised in an affectionate household, so I've had to come to terms with the fact that my mother's never going to stop me one day and say to me, "Herbie, I love you," or, "I haven't always agreed with your choices, but I respect you for having made them, and I'm proud of what

you've done with your life." I'm never going to get that from my mother in that manner, but I know she feels it. That's the love part, that's that intangible bond. Her expression of love for me was putting a roof over my head, food in my belly, and clothes on my back.

It's always been just me and my moms. I did not grow up with my father at all. I could pass my dad on the street now and probably not recognize him. He certainly wouldn't recognize me with these locks. My pops came into my life briefly when I was about twelve years old. So from zero to twelve I had no relationship with or connection to my dad, other than I knew I had his name, Quinones. Moms never said, "If only your father were here, we wouldn't be going through this." We didn't "go through" anything. I think if she had more than one child we would have struggled. But we weren't dependent on public assistance or anything like that. Moms worked, and with her it was always cash, everything cash. She put me through private school, from grammar school through my sophomore year of high school. It was important to her that I do well, although she probably couldn't articulate why it was important. It was, you've just got to go to school, 'cause it's good for you.

My moms grew up in what they call *el campo,* the countryside, in Puerto Rico. She was part of a whole wave of Puerto Rican women who were solicited to work in the factories in the States. She didn't speak the language when she came. To this day she still has a pronounced accent; when you hear her speak you know this is not a sister who was raised on Park Avenue and Eighty-sixth Street. My moms worked in the garment district as a seamstress for twenty-something years until she retired about five years ago. She worked very hard: like the postal service, girlfriend was up to go to work at sunrise, rain, snow, or sleet.

Working in the garment industry wasn't glamorous, and she knew it wasn't. She was just a sister trying to raise her little boy. She may have made sacrifices, wearing the shoes with the holes in them for six months, because her boy had to have his white shirt and tie for Catholic school, but I wasn't aware of it. Moms is one of those quiet people; she didn't whine about making sacrifices, she just did it. I don't recall any guilt-tripping. She took care of business, just like my friends' pops would get up at four in the morning with Sanitation.

Even when my mother wasn't around I could feel her presence. If I was doing something bad I would think, if I get caught doing this my Moms ain't gonna like it. So either I didn't do it or I tried to do it without getting caught. I think my record was pretty good on not getting caught. The few times I did get caught doing something, I'd plead, "Please don't tell my mother, man!" The time I got caught and she found out, she whipped my ass. Straight up! My moms beat my ass! I think if my mother were raising me today the way she raised me then, I'd be in Child Welfare every other week: "It's the Quinones file, pull it out."

I remember stealing some money once and getting caught. And she burned my hands! Burned them over the stove. I had second degree burns. That's abusive, there's really no way around it. But her attitude was, well, you stole! Fuck that, you do not burn a nine-year-old's hands. You just don't. I did it and I'm sorry. I stole the money, I am the felon, I'm the person who committed the crime. But I don't believe that the punishment fit the crime. In her mind it did. I remember walking

around with these blisters on my hands and people would gasp. Moms would say, "Yeah, and if he steals some shit again, I'll fuck him up again." I don't think she ever doubted that what she did was the right thing. I wasn't going to do it again. I think in her mind she wanted to make sure that I didn't get in worse trouble later, when the consequences would be more serious than a bruised ass or burned hands. Moms didn't play.

My moms is one of those mothers who if you saw her coming around the corner and you were doing something wrong everyone would freeze right in their tracks. I'm thirty-eight and some of my friends are in their forties, but to this day they will come to the house and sit on the corner just like when we were little kids, waiting for me to finish eating supper to go play. These are grown men and still they know, "Yo, you don't mess with Herbie's mom." She's got that gruff exterior, you know, that look on her face that tells you, fuck off. But it's just a look. If you can get beyond it you realize that there's really a warm person underneath it all.

Some of my friends have seen her soft side. Some, not all. The rest hear rumors. The ones who see her soft side are surprised, but they still proceed with caution. They don't like to get too comfortable, because she may laugh one day and the next she may tell you to go fuck yourself. So my friends always err on the side of caution.

I try to be open and friendly because of my mother; I didn't want to be like her. When I was a little boy, I would consciously do stuff that was funny to break the tension, because my mother could walk into a room — you know how some people walk into a room and light it up — Moms would walk in and the lights would go off. She could be that serious; and because you didn't know what kind of mood she was going to be in, until you found out, you had to play it by ear. And that can cause people to be uncomfortable. It was no fun being her son, to walk in behind that kind of energy. So I would do something to break that tension, and usually it was humorous, thank God. Something that has now turned out to be a profession for me.

I remember being on the *Apollo Comedy Hour* on television and not bothering to tell my mother. I was conditioned to edit certain things, because I thought they just fell on deaf ears. My aunt asked me, "How come you didn't tell your mother that you were on TV?"

"I didn't think she wanted to know," I said.

"Oh, no, she was upset!" she said. "She heard it at church!" She told me my mom was proud of the comedy stuff and the things I've done on television. I was like, okay. My aunt also told me that my mother is proud of the person I've become, even with the dreadlocks.

Last year my mother was in

the hospital because of kidney failure. She is on dialysis now and doing better day by day, but there are still times I look at her and think, that was a close one. I still deal with my thoughts and feelings about her mortality. It's an interesting transition. It's very deep to go from child to caretaker. Around this time last year she was just out of the hospital, and I was at her apartment damn near every day and sleeping over a lot. It was a tremendous strain, 'cause it was like juggling two households, mine and my mother's. There was a tremendous sense of obligation, but not guilt. I wanted to be there for my mother, because I recognized that all she had done for me she didn't have to do. There's no doubt, no doubt in my mind, that I was the priority in her life. You could say, well, damn, he's an only child, but I know only children who were dogged and abandoned. Just because you are an only child doesn't necessarily mean you're gonna get it all. There's no guarantee. You don't have to be a parent, you really don't. Obviously folks have rejected that and said, no, I'm not capable of doing this. She could have very well done that. I was there with my moms because I wanted to be there, maybe to help her to continue living. I'm big into hugs, and touching her and being there giving her my energy, I was hoping that would breathe life back into her body.

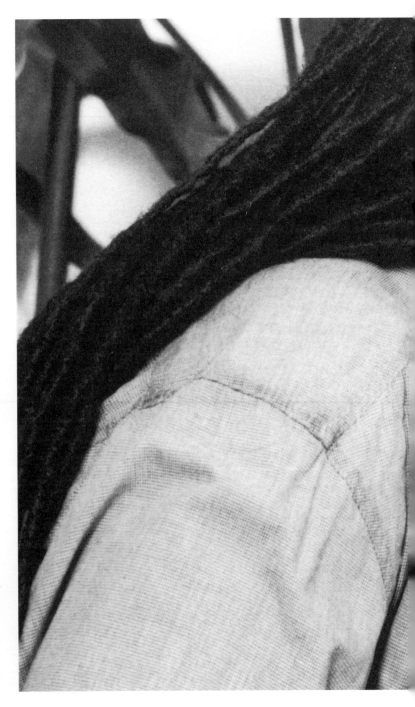

Sacred Bond

M I C H A E L   W E B B   &   R I T A   J O S E P H I N E   L E E

Unresolved childhood issues have a way of enduring in our lives. Many of the men I interviewed were still dealing with the aftermath of not being (or being) their mother's favorite, or feeling a lack of attention, or remembering actual abuse and abandonment. But no one seemed more burdened by his feelings toward his mother than Michael Webb. Although he is certain that his mother loves him, the feeling that he never received the kind of love he needed from her is something he carries with him. He has never spoken with anyone about their relationship before this interview. Some of what he expressed he has never even shared with his mother. But he wants her to understand he doesn't blame her for the decisions she has made in her life. ■ His mother, Rita Josephine Lee, is clearly proud of her son's accomplishments. He was the first in his family to graduate from high school and then he went on to earn a college degree, two master's degrees, and a doctorate. Webb is currently an educator, developing alternative schools in New York City, and is the cofounder and president of the International Youth Leadership Institute, an educational organization for youths. He serves as a consultant for many other organizations. ■ Despite his mother's words of encouragement and support, Webb has always searched for more tangible proof of her love and approval. Her words, he says, were not always supported by her actions. Their relationship underscores the never-ending urge to make things right, or at the very least, to accept imperfection.

MICHAEL WEBB
Educator/Writer
AGE FORTY-SEVEN
MOTHER RITA JOSEPHINE LEE

My mother was beautiful, she was smart, she was wonderful. I looked up to her, and all I wanted to do was be with her. I missed her so much when she wasn't there that when I got those chances to sit with her, I was in heaven. I still feel a warm feeling from those moments of sitting with her and talking, watching television, and combing her hair. She was always a pillar of strength. She made sure that no matter what, we had food on the table, we had clothes on our backs, we had a safe home. There are times when I'm sure men wanted her to go off and leave us, and she never did. However, despite these wonderful things about my mother, she tends to look at life through her own lens. I don't blame her, but she's self-preoccupied, and I can't help but feel as though I didn't get enough love from her.

I loved my mother a lot, but I hated my father because he used to beat her. My brother and I would scream and try to fight him, but my father was very strong and we couldn't do anything to protect our mother. After the first few times, my mother would lock us in another room because she didn't want us to see it, although we could hear. My mother and father broke up quite often, and whenever they did we got on the train back to Buffalo to my grandparents' house. My earliest memories were of a train, back and forth; it was almost a commute, it would happen with such regularity. I used to love those train rides, because we were leaving him. I used to be really excited about getting on that train and standing in the window looking out in the darkness, the shadows going past the window.

I didn't want my mother to go back to my father, but that's what she wanted to do. I would always feel depressed whenever they would reconcile. I think she went back because they were in love. I think they loved the things about each other that created the greatest problems between them: the independence. My mother was very independent. I think my father respected that, but at the same time he wanted to control her. My father was very headstrong, and I think that attracted my mother but was the same thing that repelled her. So they had this love-hate relationship. They broke up for good when I was about six.

We went back to Buffalo to live with my grandmother and grandfather. We had a comfortable space, and my grandmother was a nurturing woman. She and I got along fantastically. She was a pioneer, a member of the Christian Science church. She exposed me to a great many things that I would never have been exposed to as a child living in the ghetto. She went to plays, concerts, art galleries, and museum exhibits, and she would take me along. My grandmother was one of my early role models. Since my mother was young and vivacious, after she finished work as a nurse's aide, she would often have dates. So she wasn't around a lot. But my grandmother was always there. She was a nurse's aide also but she worked at night and was home all day and in the evening. I'd be right there with her.

About two years later, my mother met another man and they married. This time we got on the train and moved to Chicago. We lived in a tenement in a small two-room cold-water flat. I mean we were poor. I remember we used to get a treat when my mother would bring home bologna steaks. That's what she'd call them. They were really slices of bologna, but she'd fry them up in a pan. We lived on government subsidies, like government cheese and Spam, a little white bread. That's what we ate. And every now and then we'd get our bologna steaks.

We were in Chicago for about a year before things went sour with my mother's marriage. My mother is very stubborn, she's very headstrong, and she wouldn't back down from anyone. It was after time passed and some of the newness wore off that her independence began to grate on the egos of her men and the problems occurred. One thing would lead to another, and then before long you'd hear blows. We went back and forth to Buffalo a couple of times until my mother couldn't take it anymore. Finally, after about a year, we left Chicago for good.

My grandmother took on what you would consider a more traditional mother role. She was the one who would take time out to tend to small details like what I was wearing and what I was eating. She nurtured me in a way my mother didn't. With my grandmother I was a child. My mother more or less thought I was independent and she left me on my own. To her I was a confidant with whom she could share conversations about her dates, about what was going on at work, about what was going on in her life. My grandmother gave me the reinforcement and adulation that I didn't get from my mother. I think my grandmother had the inner security that allowed her to look outward that my mother didn't have.

93

Looking back on it, there must have been some insecurities that made my mother so preoccupied with her own needs.

This time we stayed at my grandmother's house for about five years, until my mother met another man and got married for the third time. He was a dentist. We stayed in Buffalo, but we moved to another part of town with him, until he would drink, they would fight, and he would hit her. The whole relationship broke down after a year, and we moved back to my grandmother's house.

I think my mother was with these men because she wanted to give us a father. She wanted us to have a regular family. I think she felt that she needed to validate herself with her kids, and she had to have a husband. I used to say that my mother carries a cross because she feels as though she failed her children. She feels extremely guilty, as though all the things that have gone wrong in our lives have been because of her and her failings as a mother.

Around the same time that she was married to the dentist, I entered adolescence. I stopped trying to get her attention and started rebelling against her. Whereas we used to sit down and I listened to her talk about herself, now I didn't even want to be around her. I would spend all of my time at home in my room with my door closed. She could never understand why, what caused me to change from this kid who adored his mother to all of a sudden someone who didn't want to have anything to do with her. It must have been very hard for her. I'm sure she blamed herself for that too.

I now realize my rebellion was a reaction to what I perceived as a lack of love, a lack of attention. So I created a barrier. I figured, if you don't love me, if you're not giving me this attention, then I don't need it and I don't need you. I was once talking with some friends, and she overheard me making disparaging remarks about her. She was very hurt. She told me, "I forgive you for it, but I'll never forget it." My mother is very good at making my brother and me feel guilty. She would say things like, "I know I haven't been a good mother...." And we would be disarmed. I think it was her subconscious way of affirming that there was something wrong, but not dealing with it.

When I was about fifteen she took up with a young man whose family owned property on Grand Island, an upper-class suburb of Buffalo. He built a house on his land and took us out of the ghetto. This house was a palace for us, but it was a forbidden palace. We couldn't touch anything. If we even left a cabinet open there would be a big furor. There was always tension in that house — always. My mother tried to listen to us and to show us that she cared about us, but it was a hard position for her. She would have to maintain peace, and what it came down to is that we felt she chose him over us. Then they began to fight and the violence began to escalate. It was with great glee that I finally graduated from high school and went away to college. I rarely went back. I didn't see my mother very much, and whenever we spoke, our conversations would be all about her. It was the same thing as when I was growing up. I could never talk about how I felt or what was going on with me. If I did, she would listen with a polite silence. So the distance increased.

My mother has often said she's proud of me. She's often said that she thinks what I've done is remarkable. The words have come, but the actions haven't been there. When I got my doctorate from Teachers College, Columbia University, I didn't even get a card from her saying congratulations. I didn't get any acknowledgment. It was almost as if, oh, you got your doctorate, that's fine, well let me tell you about what happened to me. That stung — for this great accomplishment in my life to be met with the same reaction that I received all my life. I can rationalize and say, "Of course she was happy I got my doctorate, of course she was proud." But her actions didn't speak that.

I often went back and visited my grandmother, or talked to her on the phone. She was the one who listened, the one who seemed to care when I told her about my problems and what was going on in my life. My grandmother died at seventy-eight, when I moved out to California in 1977, and I made a decision that I wasn't going to lose her. Her spirit would be with me forever.

As an adult, someone who has gone through his own relationships in life, I realize a lot of things that as a child I could never understand. I realize that we all have to deal with our demons. We all have to deal with the issues in our life: the lack of love, the longing, unfulfilled dreams, the bitterness about some of life's sad turns. In dealing with them, maybe the people around us catch the fallout. Maybe the people around us, especially children, don't understand that the way we act is not based upon our rejection of someone else as much as it is grappling with an insecurity. I realize that now. Intellectually I can understand, and I forgive my mother on that plane. But emotionally the hurt is so deep, I can never get rid of it. I can manage it, but the pain will be there until the day I die. My relationship with my mother has been colored by that hurt and that pain. I can deal with her in a way that helps us both to get beyond the past. But the past is still lurking very close to the surface. I'm not sure we could ever be close. I hope that it would be possible, but I don't know.

What I've looked for in relationships has been the kind of recognition, the kind of attentiveness, the kind of adoration, that I felt I missed in my mother. It's created a very great pressure on the other person, because what I look for is basically unrealistic. I've looked for a woman who is going to fulfill my need to feel wanted, to feel important, and to feel loved. I'm very quick to decide that that's not happening, so I'll strike out emotionally. I just shutter myself. It's almost like, I'm not going to get this love, so I don't need it. And of course that doesn't do anything except create a greater distance. I've been able to come to grips with it, and I've been able to talk about it much more than before. I don't see it in terms of pathology anymore. Whatever has created the pain within me has also created the strength.

I know my mother has suffered immensely. I'm happy that now in her senior years she's met and married a man who fulfills all those things that other men never did in her life. He cares about her, he doesn't try to control her. He allows her to be herself. He's there for her, and she's never had that. It took a long time, and I'm genuinely happy and also relieved, because in a sense, it takes pressure off me. If she were alone now, I would have great pressure on me to give her something more. I'm not sure how well I could do it.

I want her to understand that I don't blame her. That I understand who she is and I understand a little bit about why she did what she did. I also want her to understand that just as she was never able to get in her relationships what she needed, she was never able to give me what I needed. It wasn't because she was a bad person, because she's not, she's a wonderful person. It's just that by virtue of her own experiences and her own life she wasn't able to give to me what I have now found difficult to give to others, the sort of intimacy, the sort of compromise, the sort of giving up, that it really takes to have a successful relationship. I think she's been able to do that now.

I want my mother to know I understand why it happened. She dealt with the issues in her life the best way she knew how. It just turned out that the way she dealt with her demons was not a way that gave me the kind of love and support I needed from her. I forgive her for that. I never stopped loving her, I just stopped needing for her to love me in the way that I wanted.

97

BILL T. JONES & ESTELLA LUCIVEE WALDEN JONES

99

Conflict is an inevitable part of a mother-and-son relationship. But within that relationship is the unspoken commitment to work through conflict no matter how difficult or complicated. Of the men I spoke to, Bill T. Jones and his mother probably had the greatest hurdles to clear to find common ground. His sexual orientation, their very different lifestyles, their shared confrontational manner — all conspired to create a direct, uncensored conflict in their relationship. ■ Estella Lucivee Walden Jones, a former migrant farm worker, is a strong, God-fearing woman. For the photograph, two things were important to her, that her hat was just right and that she had a Bible in her hand. Her son grew up to be an acclaimed dancer and choreographer who has captivated, shocked, and influenced people around the world. A powerful force in the dance world, he has received numerous awards both as a soloist and with his late partner, Arnie Zane. ■ That Jones and his mother eventually did find common ground was obvious to all when they performed side by side in an act of *Last Supper at Uncle Tom's Cabin/The Promised Land,* a piece Jones created. His mother sang a song that she often led in her church in San Francisco as her son danced a solo beside her. ■ Jones and his mother seem to have found that the years of working through their conflicts have deepened their relationship. Despite their differences, this mother-son bond has kept them united and has provided both of them with the love and solace they need.

BILL T. JONES
Dancer/Choreographer
AGE FORTY-SIX
MOTHER ESTELLA LUCIVEE WALDEN JONES

In our household you never talked about sex, period. We were living at this place called Bellanger's migrant labor camp in upstate New York. It was probably around 1958, and there was a TV program on and everyone was sitting around watching it. The woman in the program was saying something about having strange cravings and not feeling well in the morning. One of my younger brothers said, "What's wrong with her?" As precocious as I was, I volunteered, "She's going to have a baby." Why did I say that? I was immediately whipped and we were all sent to bed.

I'm the tenth child of twelve. My mother had her first child at fifteen, and for the next twenty-eight years she was in some stage of pregnancy. There was always a baby in the stomach, a baby at the breast, and what they call a knee baby, one standing at the foot. When I was born, my sister was thirteen months old, and when I was a year old, my mother had another baby in her arms. We understood that she didn't have time to mess around. I never felt unloved, but my mother had her favorites. There was a pretty sister who could sing. There was the older boy, her first child, who was born on Christmas day and was like the Christ child to her. Those were the stars. The rest of us, without being too shameless, had to jockey for her affection, jockey for attention, jockey for approval. She wasn't much on giving compliments, so to get a compliment from her was something very special. The put-down or the threat of discipline was more her style. I don't know how to express how she made us feel loved, but you felt like you belonged. It was understood in the way we all smelled the same, the way my mother would handle us, absent-mindedly talking to somebody while examining to see if our noses were clean. She would touch you in a way you knew no one else in the world could.

We had seen wildness in our mother in moments when the responsibilities of motherhood were almost more than she could bear. The times when there was no food in the refrigerator, the times there was no work for my mother and father, the times they had to deal with a bureaucracy that they barely understood, often financial things, like trying to get a loan or someone wanting to repossess the car because payments had not been made. She would grieve and moan and complain, and we were the captive audience. We were frightened because her anger could turn into disciplinary action if the house wasn't clean or the dishes washed. To talk about these things is very painful. Quite frankly, when I look back on it, I wonder if that's what getting your head cracked by my mother was all about. Was it her way of pulling you in line to protect you from really getting killed, or was it that the children in the house were the one thing in the world she could control? She was a woman struggling against all sorts of forces: the white world, the economics of raising twelve kids with her level of education, being a migrant worker, and trying to manage big groups of people when she supervised the workers.

When we were of school age, there were probably twenty black people in the whole community of maybe twenty thousand people spread over fifty square miles. Any interaction between my mother and father and the community always had a racial overtone. I guess because my mother and father were raised in the South, they were always expecting to be treated as second class. My mother had a chip on her shoulder. There was a certain way the jaw was set. The gaze was steely. You were not there to compromise, you were there to confront. This was her attitude, the way she walked into the principal's office, the way she walked into the PTA meeting. She was a big woman, you realize, well over two hundred pounds most of her life. I remember there was a period in the sixties where she had a leopardskin cape coat. It was a huge thing. And she always liked big hats, big pocketbooks, and spike heels. She swayed and lurched like a big ship.

Every time she asked the school about her children, how are they doing, it was weighted, heavy; it was almost as if she was asking them to pass judgment on her. Because if her children weren't doing well, it reflected on her. And we would hear about it. We would be beat, literally beat, for bad marks. The teachers and everyone felt it when she came around. I remember at the PTA open house, my mother would be there surrounded by us, all of us required to wear our Sunday clothes. We were on our best behavior, quietly around her like she was an immense hen. We were feeling a mixture of dread that the teacher would say something that we would have to atone for later, and pride that nobody else's mother looked like ours. And of course I was very proud of her. In the way she stepped, she seemed to know something about this world that I didn't see in anyone else's parents.

Her actions taught us to be defiant. To this day I'm trying to understand my emotional patterning. For instance, where does this belligerent wild anger come from at the drop of a hat? When the anger comes, it's like blood anger. It's like, I'll kill you. That must be from my mother. She had a mixture of deep resentment at things that had been done, or things that might be done, to her and a feeling that she had to protect us in a world she was unsure of, a world that maybe was stronger than all of us.

She wanted a better life for us than she had. She had wanted to be a nurse when she was a girl of fourteen. A white doctor had offered to take her away and educate her. She'd become the maid or nanny for his family, and he would educate her and make her a nurse in exchange. Her mother refused to let her go, and the next year she was pregnant. So she wanted her children to have careers. She wanted us to speak properly. She wanted us to have the same opportunities that the white kids had. She wanted us to have our souls saved, to understand that God is in heaven and we suffer here on earth, then when it's all over we go home to the Master, who has prepared a mansion for us each. I think those were the most important things.

There is something probing in her. She's full of her biases and her shortcomings, but there is a set of values and a world-view that serves her very well. The way she looks at a person, deciding who they are as a man, who they are as a woman. The way she understands races. At dinners after performances of mine, people would be talking about all sorts of issues, the art world, politics, whatever, and my mother would turn and offer an anecdote about her church or her life, what she saw on television, what she read in the newspaper, no matter what the conversation. She'd never make any concessions. Where she sits is the center of the universe. And for a woman who has probably a sixth grade education, she holds her ground. She has a basic sense that she belongs. I find that really inspirational. Is it pigheaded? Is it arrogant? Maybe all of the above, but it's a life energy and a sense of confidence that I'm very proud to have witnessed.

When I was in college I was always bringing home friends, white friends, and I brought home Arnie, my first partner. He was different than my other friends. He was obviously an effeminate man, but I was casual and discreet with Arnie in my family's presence. My mother treated him as she did any of my friends. It would have never occurred to me to talk to my mother about my sexuality, and she found out that I was gay because I told my brothers and sisters in confidence. I was so excited about it in that heady sixties' spirit, I thought everyone else would be too. One sister was more shocked than she let on, and when I went back to college she told my mother what was going on between Arnie and me.

At that time, I wanted to go to Amsterdam with Arnie and I needed my birth certificate to get a passport. I called my mother from school to ask her to send it to me, but she refused. "You have to come up here," she ordered. "We got some talkin' to do, and anyway, you'd best stay in school." When Arnie and I came up, she confronted me about what she had heard. She asked me to come upstairs to her room, the inner sanctum, with her big bed with its four mattresses on it. She got my father to come up and they sat on the bed. I sat on the big steamer trunk she had in the room, and then she asked me, "What you doing fucking some man in the ass?" Point blank. In my mind it was just like an out-of-body experience. Knowing how religious she is, I couldn't believe that she said it. It was so direct. I was stunned. After I caught my breath I realized I didn't have to answer that question, and that's what I told her. She backed off. I don't know if she actually wanted an answer. But then my father stepped in and said, "He's a man, let him do what he needs to do." Father, as I remember him, was very nonjudgmental. But he had a bit more experience, having been out in the world. He maybe knew more about how sex worked.

My mother, on the other hand, said, "I'm your mother. I birthed you. I've seen between your legs that you're normal." She had made the connection that something had to be wrong with you physically, somehow. She was really trying to understand. She began to feel guilty, that it was her fault, and that was painful to see. But the conversation turned away from the mechanics of my sex life to how dare I consider leaving school to go to Europe. She asked me to bring the young man up to the room, and I went to get him. And there was a showdown. "My boy's nineteen," she said to him. "How do I know you're not going to take him across the water over there and leave him?"

That was the first thing she wanted to know. "You graduated, didn't you?" And Arnie said he had. "Well, my son, he hasn't graduated. He ain't got no education. You do. I am trustin' you to take care of my boy. He thinks he knows everything but he don't know nothing." I remember it was a very big moment, and Arnie rose to the occasion and said, "I give you my word." Then they actually shook hands. Arnie and I were off to Amsterdam together.

There was turbulence between my mother and him throughout my seventeen-year relationship with Arnie. But she had no choice but to deal with him, because he was strong. In some ways he was as strong as she was. He demanded respect, and he also learned to keep his distance. But I knew deep down I was never going back to identifying myself as being a Jones first. I became part of a continent of two: Bill and Arnie. My home was no longer with my mother and father after I left at eighteen. My home was wherever Arnie and I were. I'm the first openly gay person in my family, ever. All of their feelings about freaks and sissies and faggots had to be mitigated, in light of the fact that I'm gay. It was very clear that this was another type of Negro that I had become.

When Arnie got sick…that's a difficult period to remember. I told my mother, but I didn't feel that I could really talk to her about it. I didn't know who I could talk to. We turned to the gay community, we turned to friends who worked for the dance company. Arnie always prized my mother's spiritual aspects, and there are two things that happened. He went out west to do some vitamin C therapy and was within a drive of San Francisco, where my family had moved. My sister Rhodessa, to her great credit, motivated my mother and whoever else would come to go out and pray for him, sing with him, give him support. Arnie was staying in a motel, and later he said he could hear my mother and her friends coming. He said it was amazing. They came walking through the motel singing. They did a prayer service with him. My mother did her thing, and then they left. It was beautiful. It may have been a bit forced on her part, but the fact is, she did it. When he found out that he was really not going to get better, I remember him calling my mother from the hospital two weeks before he died and asking her to pray for him. Well, Arnie was not an overly religious person, but he loved that about her. He felt power in it. Maybe he wanted to feel it too.

I'm not sure if I ever had to tell my mother I was HIV positive. When Arnie was sick she could barely say the word "AIDS." I used to have fights with her on the phone during our Sunday-night conversations about saying the word rather than saying "that disease." She knew her son could be the next one. I was trying to get her to say it, and to make a point I may have said, "I could die too."

My mother didn't ask me much until after Arnie's death. Now she always wants to know, "Let me know what the doctor said." One Thanksgiving in '88 or '89, she looked at me and actually felt my chest and my arms and said, "Why, you looking good, praise the Lord, praise the Lord." She touched my ass: "You're looking good, you're looking good." She was obviously watching. That time she didn't care what I told her. She wanted to see me and feel me. She wanted to read how my health was. We have a real rapport now, and she trusts me. If I tell her it's all right, I'm okay, she says, "Praise the Lord. My prayers are being answered." Then we go on to other things.

When Arnie died, my mother and I got closer. I had seen the devil and the worst that could happen. Grief does strange things to you. My guard was down and I was open. Also around the time Arnie died, in 1981, my father died. I remember the first time that she and I truly commiserated about having lost mates. It was a very subtle conversation. She might have even instigated it by talking about grief and talking about my father. I asked her about the demons that come in the night when you are alone and grieving, and she simply said, "When they come, I just change the channel." We were sharing tips about how to survive.

She does inspire me. I have reservations about some aspects of her rearing us, her parenting and all, but her spiritual beliefs were so consistent, her values were so consistent in her life — that is special to me. She was not conflicted around the thing that to me mattered the most: How do you live in this life with courage? She was always brave. She is a courageous woman. That transmitted in a deep way. She owns the ground she stands on, and that is a difficult quality to cultivate if you don't have it. I have a special place in her life right now. The fact that my mother loves me was always without question. Now was she a cuddly, tender mother? No, not at all. But the basic love and the thought that you belonged to her was always there. It was a love that was almost more than a young man of my temperament needed.

Sacred Bond

MICHAEL HARRINGTON & LOUISE HARRINGTON

Michael Harrington was able to avoid much of the conflict that Bill T. Jones experienced because of his sexuality. Although Harrington, a gay activist, is outspoken on gay and lesbian issues, he never had to explain his lifestyle to his mother, and his mother never felt the need to confront him about it. ■ Harrington is the eldest of eight children – seven boys and one girl – who grew up in a rambling twenty-room mansion in the Hyde Park section of Chicago. His father worked in real estate and his mother was a social worker. The fact that Harrington and two of his brothers are gay was a nonissue for Louise Harrington – the important thing was that her children grow up to be productive, socially responsible citizens. Harrington has certainly fulfilled that requirement. He has spent the last ten years building a consulting firm through which he lends his expertise to nonprofit groups trying to improve the conditions in their communities. He is also one of the founders of Chicago Black Lesbians and Gays, the largest organization of its kind in the city. ■ His mother's silence about her son's sexuality can be interpreted in several different ways – as denial, as indifference, or even as approval. Harrington is convinced, not so much by his mother's words as by her actions, that she accepts his lifestyle. Her unquestioning support of his work and relationships assures him that she's proud of what he stands for and who he is.

MICHAEL HARRINGTON
Community Organizer
AGE FORTY-FOUR
MOTHER LOUISE HARRINGTON

I probably started to realize that I was gay as early as high school. I was not chasing girls, and I was not interested in other things boys are supposed to be interested in, like fighting and sports. I was interested in my studies. I didn't get harassed about being gay…because I didn't spend time telling people I was gay. I was not overt. I just knew what I was, and I knew what I liked and what I didn't. To this day, my sexuality has not been a matter of discussion at home. Not a lot of people discuss sex with their family in the first place. I certainly know in black families it's not something that's talked about. But whether or not it was discussed, I believe my sexuality was met with nothing but total acceptance by my mother.

I'm the eldest of eight kids, seven boys and the littlest, number eight, is a girl: Michael, Marcus, Mark, Maxi, Myer, Mercer, Mason, and then there's Cecely. There were a lot of people for my mother to keep track of, but she was always very organized. I remember every time we went clothes shopping, even though there were seven of us wearing different sizes, she managed to get matching outfits for us. There was a phase during which we all had Nehru jackets – lime green, orange, blue, yellow – different colors, but we all had a Nehru jacket during that part of the sixties. We would always have matching dress coats. Everybody got the same thing. And that's pretty much what she did across the board. Everybody got the same encouragement, the same discipline, the same kinds of chores. Everybody got a full plate of the same thing from my mother. We all turned out to be very different, but she was molding little Harrington kids in the way she wanted.

My mother was always concerned about being ready for the public, and we were always ready. We had to dress up to go downtown. She felt young black people have to be a little better and step-up when they go out. And she wants to be ready for company. I remember when I moved out of the house in my early twenties, I said to her, "I'm bringing my partner by." And her reaction was "Wait, I got to get the house cleaned up." So that would be the only kind of thing that you would ever hear from her, not is this person gay, bisexual, transsexual, or anything, she would just want to be ready. Manners are important to her, as is treating people the way you want to be treated.

Till this day I have never had a conversation with my mother about being gay. There was really no need to do it. I just had gay friends and I was gay with my gay friends. Now here I am, forty-four years old, so it's almost twenty-four years of "out" gay adulthood. My mother has always come to my home, been at my parties with my gay friends. My partner and I had a big Halloween party last year, and my mother showed up as Cleopatra with all of this gold and regalia on her eyes. There were about a hundred people, most of them gay and lesbian people, and my mother looked wonderful and had a great time. All of my friends know her as Louise, because I don't refer to her as my mother. She never raised us to call her Mother or Mom so we've always known her by her first name. Our relationship is more like really good friends than mother-son.

Two of my brothers are gay. They didn't come out until long after I did. I think seeing their oldest brother on TV with the mayor talking about gay issues might have given them a little bit of confidence, but again, the issue of sex and sexuality was not discussed. I think my father may have been disappointed, but he never let us know if he was or if it made a difference. My parents were concerned about major pivotal survival stuff, things that made more sense to be concerned about. The important things for my mother with her children were "Are you working?" "How come you didn't get up early enough to get to school on time?" "Did you do your home-work?" Gayness was not the issue. That you were living up to your responsibilities as a human being in this society was the issue.

First and foremost, my mother taught me self-confidence before I knew I was gay, before any kind of sexuality crossed my mind. I felt competent and confident. I was very outgoing, so I think what my mother did was give me support to be creative, to work. My mother gave me strength to be a strong person, and I appreciate that. I remember her always urging me to do more. What have you done lately? was her motto, and What time are you supposed to be at school? Only in recent years has my mother stopped calling me at eight o'clock in the morning to make sure I'm awake. She did it through my twenties and all through my thirties and does it with all my other brothers. She calls them up in the morning: Have you gotten up? Are you on your way to work, school? That's embarrassing! But I think it shows a lot about how much

she cares and pays attention. It was more important for her to call and make sure you got up for work than to worry about who you're sleeping with and what you're doing in bed.

I remember when my first lover became sick with AIDS. We were no longer together, but I ran into him when he was sick. I immediately took him into my house to take care of him. His own parents didn't. Half of his friends abandoned him. My mother would come up to my apartment to sit with him. She would show up there to do what was right. It was not surprising; it was really wonderful and great. When he finally went into the hospital, my mother was there with me day and night. She would even show up at the hospital when I couldn't, just to sit with him. This was in 1988, and God, this is '97 and people are still afraid of AIDS. My mother wasn't afraid at all. My mother simply asked me, "Are you okay?"

"I get tested regularly," I told her, "and I'm HIV negative." That's as close as we've come to discussing my sexuality. My mother is very intelligent and very well read. She was a social worker back when social workers went door to door, which they don't do anymore, to make sure babies had diapers and people had food. She was involved in a caring profession, so I guess that played a part in her sensitivity and understanding.

My mother has always been there for me. Even when we were fighting about this or that, she has always forgotten the fight and showed up to do whatever was right. I love her deeply, and all of my friends know it. I certainly read all of the horrible stories that come as a result of one's sexuality. Gay suicide is highest among teenagers. People that I talk to have gone through all kinds of inner turmoil deciding whether or not they should tell their parents. I feel very lucky.

MALIK YOBA & MAHMOUDAH YOUNG

MORE THAN DNA

There isn't much that Malik Yoba doesn't share with his mother, and in fact their ability to talk openly seems to be one of the defining characteristics of their relationship. More than anyone else I interviewed, Malik Yoba and his mother, Mahmoudah Young, interacted like peers. Their current relationship grew out of a painful past: Mahmoudah Young was forced to leave her family to escape abuse, and for many years Yoba was raised by his father. When mother and son were finally reunited, they based their new relationship on mutual respect and openness. ▪ I met Yoba and his mother at the Soul Cafe, the midtown restaurant that Yoba co-owns, and immediately I noticed that they look more like brother and sister than mother and son. Clearly they share a great deal, both personally and professionally: Young is executive manager of her son's company, Nature Boy Enterprises, a business focused on entertainment, education, and community action. She also makes sure the four-time NAACP Image Award recipient's life runs smoothly, now that Yoba has gained a great deal of visibility in his role as the tough, hip, yet sensitive J. C. Williams on the Fox Television series *New York Undercover.* A victim of street violence and police harassment as a teenager, Yoba is also a dedicated activist, using his celebrity to bring attention to youth issues. ▪ Yoba found it difficult to explain the bond he has with his mother; he says their uncanny connection goes beyond genetics. Their story reminds us that even if a man doesn't grow up under his mother's influence, it's never too late to forge a fulfilling relationship.

MALIK YOBA
Actor
AGE THIRTY-ONE
MOTHER MAHMOUDAH YOUNG

My mother and I were separated from the time I was ten years old until I was about sixteen. After my parents split up, the six kids stayed with my father. I don't know how my mother dealt with it, but I'm sure it was very difficult. I know it was especially hard for her to leave because the two youngest kids were four and two. But she felt that if she didn't leave, it would have been kill or be killed. At first I didn't fully understand what was going on and why she had to leave. I just remember it was pretty traumatic.

I got in a lot of trouble at school and around the house after that. My father was very strict, he was always very quick to administer pain – what he called discipline. I used to get beat with extension cords regularly. I remember ironing a pair of overlaps, the polyester pants everybody was wearing, and leaving the iron down on the pants. When I picked up the iron, the pants had melted onto the iron. My father would have normally punished me, but this time he just yelled, and then he broke down. "It's not your fault," he said. "If your mother was here you wouldn't be going through that." That's what I remember now at thirty-one years old, twenty years later: It wasn't my fault, it was my mother's. My father, in all his bitterness and pain, tried to paint my mother as this irresponsible, uncaring,

ruthless woman. I knew it wasn't true. There was nothing he could say or do to convince me that she was any of those things, because of this connection I had to my mother. We had this special thing, so by the time I was ten and she left, I was very sad, but I never felt unloved by her – or by my father either.

I later understood this bitterness my father had as his pain of her leaving him. In a lot of ways, my mother was almost like a seventh child to him. He treated her like a kid, because he was seventeen years older than her. I never resented my mother for leaving. I think my younger sisters did, but I understood. At first my mother was permitted to come see us, then after a while it became too difficult. I didn't really see her again until I was fourteen. I snuck out to Brooklyn where she was living. I wanted to see her because I felt there was a huge piece of my life missing.

We slowly returned to my mother as we all went through our trials and tribulations, that is, getting kicked out of my father's house. When I was sixteen, my father caught me in bed with this girl, buck naked. He felt I disrespected the house, because Muslims are not supposed to have sex before marriage. I was so used to getting beat that when he said, "Pack your shit up and get out," I said, "Can't you just beat me?" I wasn't quite ready to leave. At first he told me to take everything I had, and after a second thought he said, "No, everything you have, I bought. Leave with the clothes on your back." I had twelve bucks in my pocket, and I took my bike, my guitar, my back-pack, and the clothes that I put back on and that's it. I went to live with my mother.

It had been very difficult for her at first. My mother went to live with a friend in New Jersey and slept on the floor. During that time she was always afraid that my father was going to track her down and kill her. She did a lot to cover her tracks and was only able to contact us through friends. In a sense my mother had to create a whole new life for herself. Having been with my father from the age of eighteen to thirty-two, she didn't have a lot of job skills. She had to learn to do things for herself. When I went to live with her she wasn't in a position to support me financially. She found clerical and administrative jobs in the performing arts, but I had to work, and my older siblings helped me too. At that point they were on their own; one sister was in college and my brother was staying with her, and another sister was staying in Brooklyn with a friend of hers.

My mother was completely different from my father. He was very repressive. My friends used to call him Ayatollah. My mother to the contrary was very sensitive and always trying to find balance and equity. She always gave us the sense that if really you want to be an astronaut or an actor, you can do that. She instilled that in us long before I moved back in with her. "Anything you want to do, I'll support you," she always said, and it went a long way. When I told her I want to act, she said, "I have a friend that runs a theater company. Why don't you join? Or you can be an usher at the Negro Ensemble Company." I became an usher. She was always trying to match my dream or my vision with a reality. She still does that. The only thing that has shifted is, the little boy has evolved into a man. She has always been very supportive of just about anything I want to do. My father was never like that. "You can't do this, you can't do that" was his attitude. He believed that there's some law in Islam

that says you shouldn't make money off a God-given talent. Go figure. It never made any sense to me. There were a lot of things about the way I was raised, as a Muslim, that I just didn't believe.

My father was so rigid and repressive, and then with my mother it was like the sky's the limit. I went from this world in which you couldn't do anything, to a world of freedom. So I was a wild man. My mother couldn't reel me in. She probably has horror stories about how I used to keep her up at night because I would go out, hanging in clubs with my friends, and I would never call. She would protest, especially about me not calling her and keeping her up all night, but she also realized, what am I going to do, punish him like his father did? She basically just let me go ahead and experience things, and that really helped get me to where I am now. I guess prayers and just being patient helped her get through it, and we also had this communication going on between us. I could talk to her about anything.

At a very early age I had a lot of experience with women, older women. I used to share these experiences with my mother very candidly. I'd tell her I slept with so-and-so last night, or I slept with so-and-so's mother last night. My mother helped me understand the feelings I was having about casual sex. I remember sitting on the floor when I was about seventeen. I had had sex with some girl, and I kept touching my chest, saying, "I just feel like there's a hole." And my mother said, "You feel empty." I really didn't have the language for what I was feeling, and she helped me define what that was. It was always a good feeling to be able to just kick it with my mom like that.

I've watched the way my mother is, what she represents, and I've definitely said to some women, "You need to hang out with my mother." Not like I'm a mama's boy, but, like, "Yo, you need some schooling in class." One of the things that's always remarkable about my mother is how everyone consistently says the same thing about her. When people meet her they tell me, "Your mother is so classy," or, "She's such a queen." I call her a snob; but that's okay because there are certain things that she represents as a woman that I've taken as a standard of how women should be. For instance, chipped fingernail polish. I used to watch my mother, who had very little time, make sure the polish was either all on or all off. There was nothing in-between, ever. Whether she had to do it on the subway or on the bus, I remember her saying, "All on, or all off." I tell women – whether it's the ones I'm working with or the ones I might be interested in – "It's either all on or all off." Some of my girlfriends have totally loved my mother. Some are probably intimidated; they don't outwardly show it, but I'm sure they are, because my mother has a pretty strong presence and she can be shady if she doesn't like something. I think I am like her.

My mother and I love eating in restaurants and discovering food and culture. Once, she and I were in a restaurant in Chicago for an event I was doing. I was sitting at a table with some young people and my mother was at another table with the adults. We ordered the exact same thing, from a glass of red wine, to a crab cake appetizer, to a steak dinner – the exact same thing. She recently bought this chaise lounge for me that I noticed in a store in Washington, D.C., three weeks before she actually bought it. My mother kept talking about how she bought this thing and she hoped I liked it. I was going to work one day while the guy was delivering it down the hallway, and I knew exactly what it was. We think the same way, so we have those kinds of connections. If we start improvising a song, we often fall in harmony quickly. I might start doing some Nat King Cole and she'll just chime in, and we'll often just flow together that way. I know some of it is just DNA stuff, but there's something unique going on.

There are aspects of this whole transition to living as a celebrity that are difficult. But because my mother's a very gracious person she helps make things easier. She has the presence of mind to send a gift or a thank-you note when someone does something for me. My mother doesn't manage my acting career or my music, but she helps manage my life. She is the queen bee of the company I founded: she does everything from making sure my plane tickets are where they're supposed to be, to scheduling a dentist appointment, to representing me in a meeting. We have both learned a lot in this business of being a TV personality and making money. All of it requires a lot of focus and a lot of attention to details that I don't always have time to deal with, so I definitely need somebody I can trust.

Working together brings us even closer in some respects than she may be to my other siblings. It's a little different now as an adult, and I miss the times I used to sit down with her and talk about some girl or something. We're in a space now where we're learning together. We are almost peers. But I still defer to her for certain things, or I'll just go and hug her or put my head on her lap. I'll have her rub my head. I still do that, all 230 pounds of me. And why not — because I'm a grown man? Fuck that. I'm still her little boy.

121

WALLACE LYNCH & MERCEDES HERNANDEZ

Wallace Lynch knows how the trauma of being separated from his mother can affect a child. He was taken away from his mother twice in his young life: the first time as a result of his parents' divorce; the second time because of his mother's addiction to drugs. Lynch shared his story with me because he knows many other children are experiencing the same thing, and he knows what it takes to survive. ■ The twenty-year-old college student grew up in the Grand Concourse section of the South Bronx, a close-knit working-class community situated between Yankee Stadium and the Bronx Municipal Court. But there were pockets of trouble on what the residents there called the "dark blocks"— adjacent streets off the main boulevard where a darker side of life thrived. Lynch's mother, Mercedes Hernandez, was one of its victims. ■ Lynch is now well-protected from the rough streets of his childhood. He is currently a junior at Fordham University, and his mother is once again a significant part of his life. Their relationship has endured the disappointment, the emotional and physical neglect, and the near abandonment that resulted from her addiction. What makes Lynch and his mother truly remarkable, however, is that the trauma that threatened to destroy their relationship has actually strengthened it. When we returned to Lynch's old neighborhood in the Bronx for the photograph, the young man either held or touched his mother the entire time. As we were leaving to go back to Manhattan, he pointed to his mother and said, "This is the only person in my life who really ever loved me."

WALLACE LYNCH
College Student
AGE TWENTY
MOTHER MERCEDES HERNANDEZ

———

When my mother and father divorced she didn't have anything. My father sent my brother, two sisters, and me to live with his mother in Puerto Rico. My mother worked hard to get herself together. She tells the story about how she played bingo to help get us back. One time she actually won, and that gave her enough money, with what she saved up from working. She came to get us all by herself. It was perfect timing, because my grandmother had just died. This was the only person that I knew other than my mother. We went to live with some aunts, but it was tough because we weren't really their kids. So my mother came to take us back to live in Queens. I was three years old. I remember my mother holding me in her arms on the plane all the way to New York. I could feel this strength, this certainty that she didn't want to let me go, ever again. And she tried to do whatever she could to make me happy. I knew my mother felt like she had lost something when we were away, and she wanted to make up for it.

We lived in the basement of my mother's father's house for about six months, until we got a place of our own in a small tenement in the Bronx, a really bad part of the Bronx. My mother decided to go to school to become a dental assistant. She did this while working odd jobs in fast food restaurants and doing other menial work trying to save up as much money as she could so she could get us out of there. After about a year she got a job as a dentist's assistant, and took us to the Grand Concourse to live. I was five. The apartment was the greatest thing I'd ever seen, a two-bedroom apartment. I could see Yankee Stadium from the roof of my building. It seemed like a house.

At the time, my father paid child support but we never saw him, except maybe a couple of times. He would tell me he would come see me, but he rarely would. I remember going to a school that was right next to where my father lived. He never picked me up once. I never stayed at his house. I remember crying for my father and being upset at my mother because I felt like it was her fault that my father wasn't around. So she tried to make up for it in any way she could.

My mother was never really strict with me except when I would stay out late. She would yell out the window, "Sube!" That means come upstairs, in Spanish. So every night before it got dark my mother used to open the window and call out, "Wallace, sube, sube." And everyone on the block knew what it meant. And they used to say, "Sube, Wallace, sube." The first time my mother hit me was when I didn't go upstairs when it was time to eat. We were all playing stickball in front of the building, and she came down.

"Uh-oh," everyone said, and the game came to a stop.

"What's everybody stopping for?" I said, and turned around. Smack! Right in my face. It was a great laugh for everyone who was out there.

I always saw my mother as strong. I remember her working overtime just so I could have money for a school trip, for lunch, or things that some people might think unnecessary, like brand-new sneakers so you can feel like you're equal to your friends. She never wanted me to feel like I was inferior to anyone. She didn't want me to feel the emptiness of kids who didn't have a mother there who loved and cared for them. I think the most important thing that my mother did was to be there every day and to always assure me that I was important to her.

But when I was about nine, a lot of things started happening. My mother lost her job as a dental assistant and ended up on welfare for about a year. My brother started selling drugs and then began using them. My mother eventually got a job as a security officer and had to carry a big revolver — along with the burdens and the problems she was already carrying: my brother

had left home to live on the streets, one of my sisters left home because she had enough of New York, and my other sister had a baby.

One day I remember seeing my mother coming home late from work and seeing something different when I looked in her eyes. It was a look unlike any other. I think the years had finally caught up to her. She was at a point in her life where she started to carry a bigger burden. I didn't know what it was, but I started to see things change around the house. She didn't really speak to me as much as she used to, she just went out, I rarely saw her. When I did see her, she'd say something and then just go right into her room and fall onto the bed. Then she began missing days at work and I would wonder why.

My mother used to cook all the time. She took pride in cooking for us, putting the food on the table herself. That's how she showed her love. Then all of a sudden she just stopped cooking. She would give me money to go eat out, every day.

"Here, take this and go," she'd say. That's when I knew something was going on for sure. I looked around and I remember going into my mother's room and seeing little pink vials. I was really scared. I thought maybe they were my brother's. But in another six months, I started to see my mother deteriorate. At her prime she was about 120 pounds. Within a span of six months she went down to as little as 90 pounds. She was already petite; now she was emaciated. She never ate. Then I knew for sure she had started down a different route in her life. She was taking drugs. For the first time in my life I felt that my mother had given up. I felt she was giving up on me.

People in the neighborhood, my "friends," started to see it and make fun of me.

"Your mother's a crack head; your mother's a drug fiend," the kids from around the corner would say. You could look at my mother and know, this lady's on something. She had lost some teeth and looked really bad, but she would always hold her head up and take me wherever I wanted, knowing that people would talk. She was just strong enough to hang on to the last bit of self-respect, the last bit of confidence. I couldn't believe that it was happening. I knew my mother wouldn't just leave me to fend for myself.

I would search her room for things. I would find crack vials and drug paraphernalia, like paper and pipes. I would take everything I found and hide it from her. I used to take it out of the house. It came to a point when I would hear my mother come into the apartment sometimes just going crazy, just out of it, just strung out. And it hurt. I had never seen my mother like that. I remember us having a television, telephone, furniture, and watching them vanish. Then my own things began to disappear, my Nintendo, my toys. All the things my mother broke

her back to give me, my brother sold. My mother would just say, don't worry, he'll bring them back, but he never did. She was allowing my brother to sell things and get money for drugs. They shared the habit.

I remember hanging out on the streets more. I came in at all hours of the night. I never heard "*Sube*, Wallace, *sube*," again. I started getting into fights and doing a lot of negative stuff that now I regret. I guess I was letting out my anger. I just wanted my family to be like everyone else's. One day I got so mad at my mother for what she had done, I yelled at her, "I can't believe you would do this to me."

"You just don't understand, Wallace," she said. "You just don't understand."

I was so angry I just walked away and went in my room. I cried, because I didn't understand why she did it. I remember searching deep down in my heart, praying and crying out to God. But my mother went deeper into her hole. I felt like everything was over for me. I stopped showing an interest in school. I remember racking up about sixty absences a year, cutting classes, but never failing because I knew how to pass the tests.

It came to the point where we didn't have any food. My mother didn't have any money to give me, she didn't cook, she never shopped. I felt like I lost that mother who was there to cook for me, to keep me in line, but yet I knew that I didn't lose her completely. I knew in my soul that she was still the mother I loved so much. I knew spiritually and mentally she was there for me – I knew because she cried when I cried. I knew she was trying to escape the situation she was in, to escape from the hurt of her past. I knew deep down inside that she loved me, but the drugs were just overwhelming.

It came to the point where she lost everything. We had eviction notices coming to our door, to the place we had lived for eight years. She tried to reel back, to get things together and pay a little rent. But she had dug herself into such a hole that it was almost impossible to come out.

When I was about twelve things had gotten so bad that my father, lying on his deathbed from cancer, requested that I be separated from my mother because she was an addict. He had known what she was going through but he didn't do anything to help. He never tried to take me to live with him while he was alive. I guess he figured while he was dying he would try to make sure that at least I had an opportunity somewhere else. So I went to stay with an aunt of mine. They knew that I didn't want to leave my mother. I remember my aunt saying, "Come with us to stay for the weekend," and the weekend becoming a week, the week becoming two weeks. Then after about a month I realized that I wasn't expected to go back home. My mother still had some time left on the apartment before the eviction, so I took my bag of clothes and went back to her.

She was so happy to have me back. "I'm going to make things better," she said, and told me she had missed me. But I could see in her face that it was just not going to work. She knew she couldn't really give me anything, and giving me up was necessary because it was best for me.

"I love you so much, Wallace," she said. "But it's just better for you to go with your aunt. She has more to offer. Don't worry, I'll be back to take care of you." I was just really feeling for her at that moment. I knew I wasn't going to see my mother for quite some time.

She was evicted from her apartment, and actually went through a rehabilitation program. For six months she had to cut off all outside contact as part of the program, and I didn't speak to her. She called me at the end and told me she was off the stuff, but I never lived with her again. I lived with my aunt until I graduated from high school. After she had gotten herself together, my mother and I both realized that it was better for me to stay where I was.

My mother now lives by herself. She doesn't even live in an apartment, she just rents a room. She's very poor. She still works in security. My mother has told me a lot about what she went through. She has been sober for the last seven years, has gotten an education, and has become wise through experience. She is now like a sister to me. I call her Mommy and give her respect — I shut up when she says to shut up — but she's like a friend; we can talk about anything.

One time my girlfriend and I were sitting with my mother in a Burger King. We were talking about colleges, and she just started crying.

"Mommy, what are you crying for?" I asked.

"I'm just so proud of you," she said. "I'm sorry for all those years that I did wrong. I just want you to understand how proud I am of you." She sat there shedding tears and told me, "With you I feel like I started something, went to sleep for eight years, woke up, and it was done, without me going through to the finish. But I am so thankful, because what I woke up to see was everything I prayed for."

She told me she was sorry, not only because of the drugs, but for the time that she missed, my high school years, for not being there for me. She explained to me she did the drugs to try and escape; to escape the hurt and the pain that she had felt because of her mother, her family, my father leaving her; to escape the feeling of failure. She felt that everyone had turned their backs on her. She said she realized in the aftermath of all the problems that she had done something she thought she would never do: turn her back and leave her children alone. That's why she turned *to* something. It was too overwhelming for her.

Now she doesn't miss anything. She's been to every big event of mine since she's been out of the program. She still wants to be there for me every day and to cook for me every night like when I was younger. She knows that my needs have grown bigger and that she could never afford to pay for everything like she used to, but she tries to help me when I don't have any money, and with books for school. No one else was there for me but my mother, and I feel this special bond to her that can't be replaced. She shows me that you have to have a heart; that's what people are going to remember about you. One of her favorite sayings is "God don't like ugly." And it's true.

I was angry at times because I always felt like, why me. But then sometimes you got to look at things like, why not. What my mother has always shown me is you can beat the odds. The odds for my mother weren't great, and at least I had a mother who loved me. Some people don't have that.

I wish I was lying to you right now. But the reality is that things happened that way, and I'm not ashamed of it, because it just made me understand that in life you can go over any boundary that's put in your way. My mother made some mistakes in the past, which contributed to where she was in her life, but she was able to say, "Look, I got to feed these kids." Then when things went seriously wrong and she couldn't work them out, she was able to lose her pride and say, "I have to give them up." And that's why I am no longer upset at her for doing what she did. She made the smartest move when she gave me up. If you ask any businessperson, if they are incurring losses in their business, what are they going to do: keep it and drive it all the way to the ground? or give it to someone else who can take care of it, who can run it to make sure the business survives.

My mother did what was right.

131

D O R I A N   W A Y N E   L E W I S   &   S A N D R A   G R E A V E S

The responsibility of taking care of our parents is something most of us are likely to face one day. When the time comes, most of us are unprepared for the emotional and financial toll of becoming, in effect, our parents' parents. A number of men in this book are at that stage in life already, but for no one else was the shift into the role of caregiver as abrupt and bewildering as for New York City detective Dorian Lewis. ■ A thirteen-year veteran in the police force, he has seen his share of human tragedies on the job. But none of his duties — from monitoring gang activity to providing security for the mayor of New York — have taken more out of Lewis than caring for his mother, who fell victim to an aneurysm at the age of forty-seven. ■ His mother, Sandra Greaves, once asked her son to make sure she never ended up in a nursing home. She worked as a nurse's aide in a geriatric hospital and had seen firsthand the kind of isolation, loneliness, and despair many of her patients experienced. Lewis has had to make heart-wrenching decisions as he's tried to reconcile his mother's wants and needs. The experience has changed both of them immeasurably, but the love between them survives, and Lewis remains a devoted son. He remembers his mother building his self-esteem. He remembers her friendship. Her hugs. In the end, this is the only way a son can repay his mother for all the love and care she has given him.

DORIAN WAYNE LEWIS
New York City Detective
AGE THIRTY-THREE
MOTHER SANDRA GREAVES

My mom used to tell me things like "I love your skin color, I love your hair; I wish mine was like yours." I think she said it to make me feel good about myself. Complexion was a big issue in my mother's family. They were from Panama and all had very fair complexions, the long hair, the whole bit. Both of her siblings, her sister and her brother, married white. So my cousins are of mixed race. I don't look like the rest of her family. I look like my father, dark, with kinky hair. I can remember going to a family reunion, and I was the only one there who looked like me. My mom must have believed that I didn't feel like I was very much a part of the gathering, and she was right. But my mom always made me feel a greater sense of worth by telling me looking the way I do is just as good, if not better.

When my mom married my dad, it wasn't a popular marriage. She is Hispanic and my father is African American. My mom rebelled, maybe not purposely, but she met a black man, judged him for himself, and fell in love. And she then had me. To my mother, the sun rose and set on me. I have a younger brother, fourteen months younger. She worked real hard to make both of us feel loved, but I feel like I was singled out as the favorite. She used to call me her number-one son. I think one of the reasons was that I was old enough to understand what my mother and father were going through. They divorced when I was nine, and until she remarried, I felt like I was the man of the house. But she always tried to bridge the gap between me and my father. She told me, "Whatever happened between us was between us. Love your father no matter what, and work at the relationship." So I always had a healthy relationship with my father, I think because of her.

My mom was the greatest friend anybody could have. I used to work midnights at Gracie Mansion doing security for the mayor's house. I worked the wee hours, Saturdays, Mondays, whatever, I worked them all. There wasn't really anybody I could talk to at the time, but any hour I would call that woman, any time, any hour, she would wake up and we would have a conversation. I could wake her at four in the morning, cutting her sleep by an hour, and she would never hang up the phone. We would talk until it was time for her to go to work. It was never, I'm tired, I don't feel like talking.

I moved into my own apartment when I was twenty-five, but my mother never came to visit me in my new place. She didn't drive and it was easier for me to go see her. One day I decided to pick her up from work, at the geriatric hospital she worked in as a nurse's aide. She was so proud that I came to get her. I took her out to dinner, and we had a nice piece of fish. I'll never forget it. It was really, really good. I brought her back to my apartment and we had coffee and just talked and laughed. Then I drove her back home. I couldn't wait to do it again. But I never got the chance. About two weeks later, my mother got sick.

My mom had always suffered from headaches. She would have to stay home from work from time to time. Then she started to get high blood pressure, when she was about forty-six. One day when she was visiting my grandmother, my mom was in the shower and felt a pop in her brain and in the back of her neck. She got dizzy, and was rushed to the hospital. They thought she had suffered a minor stroke, but they misdiagnosed it and sent her back to my grandmother's. She got sicker, and went to another hospital on Long Island, where she fell into a coma. So she actually had two aneurysms. After she came out of the coma the first time she was pretty much okay, a little out of it, but okay. But then the second time she became...well, she became like a vegetable.

I thought she was going to die. The doctors could not pinpoint where the bleeding was, but if they didn't find it in time she could die. They even gave her the last rites. So I took the X rays

to a neuroradiologist in a teaching hospital in the Bronx where I used to work, and he found it immediately. He arranged for her to go to another hospital and have an emergency operation, which went on for hours. The doctor said he almost lost her on the table, and that my mom was going to have marked damage that would never be reversed. And that's her situation.

Everything I did, taking the X rays, moving her to New York City, going ahead with the operation, was very unpopular with my mother's side of the family. It was a battle every step of the way. I didn't have a lot of strength. I smoked myself into oblivion; I fell out of a relationship; I couldn't focus on work. The whole process was the most stress I had ever experienced, but I had to take charge, I had to make decisions. This was my mom. This was the woman who when I was young took care of me and my every little ailment. Whenever my brother and I were really sick she would

take us to the hospital. She was there, arguing and making sure things were done. This is just the way she was. We were her babies and she was going to make sure we were okay. She was very hands-on, take charge. Now it was my turn.

My mom is in a nursing home in Brooklyn, about ten blocks from my job. I see her once a week or every other week. It's not easy. She knows who I am, that helps, but she can't follow a conversation. She can't feed herself, she can't get up, she can't walk. She just lays there. My mother used to work in a geriatric hospital, and one of the things she always said to me was, "Don't you ever send me to a nursing home. No matter what." But there was just no choice. It was very, very hard, but it was a decision I had to make. I just figured that I would find the best nursing home available. And I would make it near by, so that I could monitor what they did. And what they don't do.

My mom was always a lady. She used to have beautiful hair, she always wore makeup, her nails were always done. I mean she was a pretty woman. Now she doesn't look anything like that. She has no color, her hair is chopped very short. The staff at the nursing home puts makeup on her and it looks like hell. She looks like a doll. She smiles, she cries, she smiles, she cries. She laughs, she cries. Part of that is a reaction to the medication; part of it, I think, is she's in and out of some sort of lucidity. One minute she might have an idea of what's going on and then a minute later she's lost. Every now and again she has said things like "Why is this happening to me?" Then she'll say something like "I've got to go to work," or "I had a hard day at work."

One time she had a seizure while I was feeding her. She has them all the time, but I had never seen one. I knew what to do, but I didn't do it fast enough and she bit her tongue. She had a spoon and food in her mouth, and my concern was she would choke. I broke down after that, but not until I left. I feel that my mom is gone. She's there, but only a thread of what she was. She's not the same person. I mean, as horrible as it sounds, sometimes I think it might have been easier if she had died. Don't get me wrong, I want to see that she's taken care of, but she's not the same person.

It's a tumultuous thing. I have to get up the nerve to go. There are times when I say I'm going and I put it off. But I know within a week I'll get the hankering to see her, to see the twinkle of the eyes and hope there's the chance that she knows I'm there. Even though she's able to say "Dorrie," even though she's able to say "I love you," even though she's crying, someone will ask her the next day if I came, and she'll say, "No, I haven't seen Dorian in months." But still it is a way of touching her, seeing her. People who have lost their parents aren't able to do even that.

She's still there and she still needs me. I don't expect a miracle. I don't believe in them. I don't think one day she's going to snap out of it. But I can't help feeling like I have been robbed. I'm a cop so I liken it to that. Am I selfish? Am I greedy? I miss my mom. I miss her company, the conversation, the laughing. One thing my mother always did was hug. And I took that on; I love hugs. I miss her hugs.... I just long for the moment when I hug my mother and she can hug me back.

AUTHOR'S NOTE: On June 23, 1998, Sandra Greaves passed away in her nursing home bed in Brooklyn. My heartfelt sympathy goes out to Dorian, his brother, Vernon, and the Greaves/Birnel family. This story is in her loving memory.

Sacred Bond

RUSSELL WOOD TORRES & DOROTHY ANN TORRES

Assuming the role of caregiver for a parent is a crucial rite of passage — one that Russell Torres, like Dorian Lewis, had to face prematurely, when his mother was diagnosed with cancer. During the time of her illness, Torres was already in the middle of another rite of passage: the momentous shift from adolescence to adulthood. It was not until years after his mother's death that Torres finally realized not only that she had missed the chance to see the fruition of her hard work in raising him, but that his preoccupation with becoming a man had prevented him from giving her the support she needed at a critical time in her life. ▪ Torres never expected talking about his mother to be so difficult, and he apologized for breaking down several times during our conversation. There are many things that he never got to say to his mother, and those unsaid words still haunt him. All of the things he dreamed of doing for his mother will remain unfulfilled. Although nearly ten years have passed, he still feels pain at the thought of his mother's missing his graduation from college and law school, and now his accomplishments as an associate producer for CBS News. Torres knows, however, that she would be proud of the man she raised. ▪ Torres took us to his mother's burial site — a place he visits once or twice a year to let his mother know that their love remains intact, and that his mother, Dorothy Ann Torres, continues to inspire him.

RUSSELL WOOD TORRES
Associate Producer
AGE TWENTY-EIGHT
MOTHER DOROTHY ANN TORRES

My mother was an extremely beautiful woman, petite, with a glow about her. She had a light complexion and long hair, sort of the mulatto look that is very common in Richmond, Virginia, where she was raised. She was a very classy woman, but cancer turned her into half of herself. It took her weight, her hair, her movement. It slowly but surely took her life. I had lost my grandmother and my great-grandmother to cancer, so when I went into my mother's hospital room and she said, "I have cancer," everything just sort of broke. I knew what it meant. My mother, my protector, my guide, the source of my comfort, would be taken from me.

At all times my mother wanted the best for me. She always impressed on me that I was the most precious thing in her life. Anything I wanted, if it was within her means or humanly possible, she made it happen. As simple as it sounds, if I wanted a toy she would get it for me. Whether it was music lessons, taking a trip, or tutors to make sure that I attended the premier public high school in Philadelphia, she made it happen. To this day I don't really know how she did it alone. My father died when I was two. They were never together. I guess she scrimped and saved. The most she ever made in a year was about $27,000. But she purchased her own home. We had a car, a Cadillac. I never knew my brother and me to want for anything.

But it wasn't all great. She was a factory worker on a bacon assembly line, and during the mid-eighties recession, Oscar Mayer laid her off. I was about fifteen. She lived on unemployment and severance pay for as long as she could, then went on public assistance. She got $180 a week in assistance and food stamps. I remember she went out and bought a typewriter, and every day she would comb the classifieds and send out resumés on top of resumés.

But my mother wasn't employable. She didn't have a high school diploma. So she went back for her high school equivalency, went to junior college and also secretarial school. This was before back-to-work programs. I can remember her sitting at the dining-room table and having problems with fractions. Imagine being a woman in your late thirties and having to go back to school to get your high school diploma, and learning fractions and algebra and all those things after you have been living without them for years. But she did it. She went from being unemployed and on welfare to going back to school and totally changing careers. Now think about that sort of mind-set. For her to stretch beyond her experience, to go back to school and better herself, is really something. When I think about how she did it with two boys and herself, that is a constant source of inspiration for me, especially when I think something is beyond my ability.

I learned her work ethic, that you just have to get out there and work. If she hadn't, there would have been two hungry kids. I saw her strive and want more. I learned that there was more. She instilled in me an unshakable belief that I would go to college and even on to law school. I think one of my mom's proudest moments was when she saw me off to college, a ritual that was not part of our family history. It was moving one more step above where we were in economics and in education level, and that's why she was pushing me. And oh man, she was just so proud, so proud. She could now say she has a son who she poured her love and all of her heart into, and it produced fruit.

I came home from college for break and I had a new attitude, affirming my manhood. My mom had bought a new car and wanted to go to Richmond. We had gone to Richmond every summer, but this year I said I wasn't going. I was sort of crushing it for her, since now I could share in the driving, and most important, she wouldn't be going by herself. Then the next morning – I'll never forget it – my mom woke up early

and she wanted to go to the supermarket. We would always go together so I could help her with the bags, but this morning I didn't feel like it, because I had gone to sleep really late the night before. She had just about had it with this sort of "young buck becoming a man" thing. I told her I was an adult now and was not into the supermarket thing. So she left huffy and puffy about eight Saturday morning. When she came back from the store, she woke me up again to help her with the groceries. What she didn't tell me was that when she was backing out of the garage that morning she ripped the side mirror off the car. I came outside and saw the mirror.

"I guess you won't be going to Virginia after all. You gotta get your mirror fixed," I said matter-of-factly.

She had about enough of my attitude and exploded. "You are not the father in this relationship! I pay the bills around here!" She told me in so many words: This is my house. Since you think

you are so grown, when I come back I want you and everything in this room packed up and out of here.

She left. This brings tears to my eyes now. She came back an hour later. I was sitting in the same spot. I heard her coming up the stairs. "You still here?" she said coldly.

I opened my mouth to say, I don't have anywhere to go, but I just started crying. It didn't even faze her. A day or two later we got through that and she told me she was still in charge. The one thing she always said that I will never forget was "I am the mother and the father." At times she was the mother, the one who encouraged and comforted, the person you could lay your head on her shoulder and she'd wrap her arms around you, the person you could crawl into bed with when you were scared to sleep in your room by yourself. But at the same time she was the stern disciplinarian. She realized she was a woman raising a young man and she had to temper that young man. She had to let him know too that she was still the head of the household, that I had to respect that.

That day, she developed a headache, which became a persistent headache. She went to get it checked out and found she had a tumor near the back of her eye. After a biopsy and a series of tests it was found that the tumor was caused by lung cancer. She soon lost the sight in one eye and became dependent on me.

I had to deal with a lot of guilt. I thought I caused the headache. I thought the headache caused the tumor that made her lose her sight. And there was one other thing that I had to address: I was still going through the "I am a man and out of the nest" phase. I was eighteen or nineteen. We were going to the doctor in Center City. She needed me to walk arm in arm with her down the street to help her. And I was still adjusting. I can remember thinking, "I don't want to walk arm in arm with you. This is embarrassing."

I think back on that and I wish could return to my mother a little bit of what she gave me. I had to blame it on youth to get beyond the guilt. When we are young we do stupid things. If I had the opportunity now, I would carry her on my back.

There is a song my mother taught me in church, "Angels Hover around Us." It says that angels guide us and keep us from harm. There are times when I look in the mirror and notice an expression or a smile, and I see my mother. She is still my protector and my guide. She's not God, but she is my angel. I still feel that pleasant spirit about her, in me.

PAUL CARTER HARRISON & THELMA HARRISON WEATHERS

LITTLE MEN

Losing a father is just as devastating to a family as losing a mother. Three of the men I interviewed lost their fathers at a young age, and in each instance, the boy's role in the family was unavoidably altered. Paul Carter Harrison was the youngest of the three when his father died. Yet even at the age of seven, he accepted his new status as the man of the house and his mother's protector like an adult. He says he and his younger brother became his mother's "little men," armed with a new sense of responsibility for their mother's well-being and happiness. ■ Harrison describes his mother, Thelma Harrison Weathers, as a genteel woman, who loved Dinah Washington and ballroom dancing at the Savoy. But when her husband died her life changed profoundly — she had to work harder to hold the family together and to continue providing a comfortable life for her two sons. She worked as a managerial assistant for the city housing authority, relied on extended family, and took advantage of the resources of the city to give her children what they needed. ■ Harrison is now an award-winning playwright, the author of several books, and a professor of theater. He is currently writer-in-residence at Columbia College in Chicago. It took Harrison many years to let go of his mother, and the way he describes their relationship poignantly illustrates the lasting sense of responsibility a son feels toward his mother, particularly when she's on her own. It also illustrates the deep satisfaction a mutually supportive relationship can bring.

PAUL CARTER HARRISON
Professor/Playwright
AGE SIXTY-TWO
MOTHER THELMA HARRISON WEATHERS

My mother was still a very young woman, only twenty-seven, when my father passed away. He came home from work one day, had a heart attack, and never recovered. He was only twenty-eight. Right before his funeral I looked at my mother and said, "We're going to the funeral, but don't cry." She said, "Okay," and cried on her own later. That's when our relationship changed. I felt that the responsibility to protect my mother fell on me. I was only seven, my brother a year younger, and we both knew that suddenly we had a new role to play. We literally became the "little men."

My mother made the transition immediately after that, went right back to work and set up the household for us. My brother and I went to Public School 113, right around the corner from our apartment in Harlem. The first thing the principal said to my mother after my father died was, "Well, you have these two boys. Clearly you want to go on welfare, don't you?" My mother said, "Of course not, I have no reason to." She was a very skilled woman. She worked for the federal government on its clerical staff at the time, and there was no reason for her not to work. The school administrators were afraid that because she would be working, my brother and I would go unsupervised. But Harlem was a nurturing place then and she had a very close-knit family, including her brother, her sister, and her sister's children. The fact that there was no man immediately in the house did not mean that we didn't have role models. We were never at a loss for some kind of male identification. We had older cousins and uncles on both my mother's and father's sides of the family. They all promoted a certain course of behavior to enlarge our responsibilities as men. In certain ways it might have been even better, because you got the influence from three or four different sources as opposed to one. So my mother never really felt that she had to find another father for her children, like some women do.

Still, there was always the question of my mother dating. Being quite a lovely woman, you would think men would have been falling at her knees. And they would have if she wanted that. But she was always very independent. She never had a serious affair with anyone. She was never one to even go out with people; my brother and I would go out with her. At family get-togethers, it was always Thelma and the boys, even up to our teenage years. So Thelma and the boys would travel together and we would dance together. We were her boys. She has always referred to my brother and me as her lambs. Everyone in the family finds this very amusing, because we are hardly what you would call lambs.

My mother was also a drill sergeant. She had a very clear sense of proportioning what the responsibilities of her boys would be. She would say, okay boys, I'm going off to work; you have these responsibilities. At a very young age we had to learn how to cook, sew, clean, wash and dry the dishes every night after dinner, the things housewives of that time would normally do. When she would do the inspection, they had to be done. Every Friday we had to go out and buy fish. On Saturdays we would do the major shopping with her and bring the groceries home.

The other thing my mother did as a drill sergeant was make sure we were in the house by five-thirty. "I get out of my office at five o'clock," she told us. "When I come out of the subway at 110th Street and I turn that corner, I don't want to see you boys out on the street." We had to be in the house. We would look up the street and see this particular gait coming down the street and the two of us would go right into the house. Even in the summer, until we were about eleven we had to be in the house and prepared for bed by seven o'clock in the evening. We

lived on the ground floor of our building, and all of our friends would be outside our window laughing and teasing, "Carter and Ken, you guys want to come out and play?" We were in our pajamas, talking to them through the window. Very rarely did we get caught outside. We didn't want to experience our mother's wrath.

When I was fourteen I remember my mother wanted to give us a spanking about something. As she started to come down on me, I looked her in the eyes and stopped her hand. The spanking didn't go any further than that. Then I realized what I was doing and immediately withdrew. My mother looked at me and we both cried. Both of us realized she could no longer do that. At fourteen I was physically stronger than she. But I also knew from that moment on that I would never do anything to make her feel impotent again. I think that to this day there are certain things my brother and I do to protect our mother from anything that offends her sensibilities.

I lived in Europe for about ten years, and I remember that when I first went there as a twenty-five-year-old I had no accountability to anyone except myself. With my newfound freedom, I could do the most reckless things I wanted. But every now and then I would encounter situations that I knew were going over the edge. When confronted with a situation like that, I channeled my mother's sensibilities; I felt the embargoes and sanctions that she would have imposed. Her level of principle and integrity has carried me a long way.

In my adult life, I see my mother less, but there has always been contact. Several years ago my mother's brother, who had been living with her, passed, so for the first time my mother was living alone in New York City. Around that time, she ran into a man she had known for many years while working at the New York City Housing Authority. He was living in South Carolina and his wife had died. We always joked with my mother, saying she had to do something more than pull her hair back into a bun if she wanted to ever catch a husband. Then this one day we were laughing about it and she said, "Well, there's a man I know who wants to marry me." My brother and I thought it was funny and laughed. We didn't believe it.

"I'm not joking," she said.

"Of course not," I said. "Everyone's walking up to you these days making a proposal."

"No," she said. "But this man did propose to me." We stopped laughing. She was serious.

There was another time, when my brother and I were about ten and eleven, that an army staff sergeant living in Europe wanted to marry her. He was a very handsome, heroic-looking man. Every time he would come to see my mother, he would bring flowers and a box of chocolates "for the boys." After

he proposed to her, my mother called me and my brother together. She asked us, "Boys, the sergeant has asked me to marry him, what should I do?" We told her, "We don't want another father." So she wrote him a letter and told him the boys don't want it. And that was it. She didn't do it.

When she next broke the news about getting a proposal, it was a shocker even for my old jaundiced sensibilities. My mother was in her mid-seventies. She called me every other day for a month, asking me, "What should I do? I've got to tell this man something." My first reaction was say yes, but then I had to go through some adjustment. In a way, my brother and I were like her boyfriends. She had to go through the boys first before she did anything. Things we took for granted, like her coming up to Chicago to visit me or taking spontaneous trips to Europe with the family, I realized, we would no longer be able to do. We would have to be careful not to impose ourselves on her time or interests, because she would have a husband. It would no longer be that simple to say, Mom, let's meet and go to lunch or dinner. She would have to first check with her husband. There would be changes in our relationship, but I realized things had also changed for my mother. Her support system had broken down. Friends were dying, her siblings were gone. She was pretty much alone. I was all over the place and my brother was also, so we didn't get to see each other as much. So here was a possible companion for her, someone who she could deal with because she had known him for more than twenty years. It made sense. I was quite moved by the idea.

"Go on," I said. "Marry the man. It's all right." They have now been married for seven years. I'm sure it went down only because we approved. As it turned out, my brother and I gave her away at the wedding ceremony. We walked down the aisle with her and gave our mother away. We now knew we had to share our mother's affection with another man.

Sacred Bond

M O M   R U L E S

Like children in more than 60 percent of African American households, Victor and Richard Stams grew up without their father at home. Their father's abandonment has left its emotional scars on the two young men and has fundamentally altered their relationship with their mother. Watching their mother raise them alone taught the Stams brothers some hard lessons about responsibility — responsibility to themselves, to their families, and to their mother. ■ They live with their mother in a high-rise on Chicago's South Side. When we met, Richard, the elder brother, barely said a word until we sat down for the interview. Victor, by contrast, was animated from the moment I arrived. Both of them, however, spoke passionately and at great length when the subject turned to their mother and the support she has always given them. Though the brothers have chosen significantly different paths in life, they share a sense of purpose and accountability. Victor's goal is to become a doctor, and Richard is focused only on being as good a parent to his child as Marguerite Stams has been to him. There has been a lot of give-and-take in their relationship with their mother; there has also been a lot of struggle. But their mother's commitment to her sons has had its lasting effects and imbued them with a sense of security. ■ Both brothers struggled to find an adequate way to express their appreciation for their mother. They both rely on her guidance and strength, and have inherited a sense of responsibility that shapes their values as well as their actions.

RICHARD & VICTOR STAMS
Housekeeping; College Student
AGE TWENTY & SEVENTEEN
MOTHER MARGUERITE STAMS

RICHARD: I just became a father. It still hasn't really hit me yet. But there is one thing for sure, I want to be there for my child because I know how it is to be without a father. When you're young and your parents are going through a divorce, they both try to pull you in their direction. I tried to listen to both sides, but in the end, my mom was the one who was there for me, and my father just up and bailed. I don't really consider him my father anymore, especially because of the things I saw him put my mother through, things I don't think I should have seen. One night when I was a shorty, my father just tripped out. I saw him damn near beat my mom in my face. My mom had on a pair of red shorts and a plaid shirt. We were sitting down, and I don't know, they started arguing and he just went crazy. My mom was balled up on the couch in a way like she didn't want to get hit by him. He grabbed the left pocket on her shorts and just ripped them off of her, then yanked her shirt. I'm sitting there crying. I'm looking at my mother crying. I felt so helpless, and I went to get help. I just hate the fact that I was so young I couldn't do anything. Anytime I see my mom crying, I think about that incident and it just hurts me all over again.

VICTOR: I realize my father made a lot of mistakes, and to a degree, he shouldn't be forgiven. But growing up we didn't know much about my father's medical past and history. I was about eight when my mother and father were going through a lot of their problems. When he left us, she wondered what happened. My brother and I were wondering too. It's just recently that he's started calling and that we found out from his doctor about his past. My dad was in the Vietnam war, and he was shot in the head and the ankle. One shot shattered his ankle bone, and he has a metal pin there. His doctor said that he clung to alcohol as an outlet for a lot of pent-up feelings and emotions. He left us to get help. I was mad at my dad, but after I found out about this, I understood. It is harder for my brother. My mother's coming to grips with it now but still feels as though that was no reason for him to leave us.

RICHARD: When I was real young my mom tried to keep her problems from us. She didn't want to show us that she was sad or hurt. I think she felt that she had to be strong for us, that she couldn't let us see her crying. So she just tried to tough it out. But over the years there were times when she needed somebody to fall back on. I knew I couldn't do anything, but I would always tell her, "Mom, I love you," so I could see that smile on her face again, just so I could make sure it would be all right. I tried to be there for her, but I don't think any parent wants to show their kids that they are hurting. I think my mother covered that up pretty well, considering she was raising me and my brother by herself.

VICTOR: I know there's a lot of pressure on her, being a single parent and me getting ready to go off to school. Sometimes I wonder how she manages it all. I'll walk by her room late at night and I'll see her in her room, crying. That makes me feel bad, but there isn't too much I can do about it. There are a lot of things she doesn't share with me. How can I really be there for her if I don't know what she is going through? I try to do little things to make it easier on her; she'll come home and dinner's prepared for her, the house straightened up. And I try to keep myself out of trouble in school, so she won't have to take time off from work and come up there.

RICHARD: Mom was always there to help me out, and I'm not even talking about financially, I'm talking about being there to listen to me. Just somebody to hear what I'm saying. There were some things, though, a son just can't talk about with his mother. With those things it was important to my mom that I got the right guidance from a man instead of me talking to any

old body. There were a couple of people in church who I could talk to when I needed a male point of view, or when I couldn't talk to my mother. I knew my mother was going to them, saying, "Talk to Richard." I would have never approached them myself. They would come up to me and say, "Hey, how's it going, what's going on in school? How are you and your mom getting along?" I would think, hold on, how did all this come about? I knew my mom was telling them to talk to me, and over time I built up trust in them. Now we can talk about anything. I can tell them point blank what's going on.

VICTOR: My mother's pretty much all I have, because I don't have a stable father figure in my life. She's my emotional support, financial support, and pretty much everything else. There are some things I really can't share with her. Those are the times when I go to Father Shaw, the pastor of our church. But most things I can share with my mother. She is good about giving

advice about the ladies. She gives me secrets and tips on what they want and how they feel about things. One of the things I'm not proud to say, though, is I can't have girl company in my room with the door closed, even when my mother's here. I'm about to turn eighteen, and I'm looking at this rule like, something's got to give. This is going to be another thing that she's going to think I'm rebelling against. It's going to be a problem, count on that, it's going to be a definite problem.

RICHARD: My mom had a lot of patience with me even when I was going through my rebellious years, hating everything. I know I put my mom through a lot. It started my senior year in high school. I used to be out there just anytime of the night with my friends. My mother must knew anything could happen. I was also going through a stage where I was tired of school. I would go to school whenever I felt like it, or just blow everything off. Nobody could tell me anything. It was my way or it was no way. I hated my mom at the time. I was telling her, "I don't love you," and all this other stuff. We went to counseling. It was bad. I know I hurt my mom, but I was going through a thing.

After I graduated, my relationship with my mother kept getting worse. I told my mother straight out that I wasn't going to college and I wasn't going to work. "If you don't go to school," she said, "you have to get a job. It's either or!" I told her, "I'm not going to do anything." That's when she gave me the boot: "Well, it's just best that you pack your bags and go. Get out!" I went to live with my aunt for a year, but before I left, my mom said, "I'm going to help you find a job." I knew she still cared when she told me to get out and in the next breath said she would help me find a job. I knew she was still loving me. She told me that nobody else was going to give me money. "Money isn't just going to fall into your pocket" is what she said. "You need a job and I'm going to help you." When I was on my own I realized I had to take care of myself and that things don't come free. I had to pay my aunt rent. After my mom put me out of the house, I finally wised up and we started talking again. I knew my mom was still there for me.

VICTOR: There is a lot of pressure, because I try to live up to the goals and aspirations my mother has set for me. It's almost like I'm leading a double life. I don't want to let my mother down by not going to school, by not being the best person I can be. I don't want to follow in my brother's footsteps and have a child at this age. I rebel sometimes, because I look at things differently than my mom would. What I think I'm doing to make myself happy, she considers rebelling. There was a young lady who I spent all my time with. My mother felt that I was slacking in my studies and falling behind in school, which I was. I guess looking back on it now, I can see where I was going wrong, but I didn't consider it rebelling. My mother did. She knows what could happen and I know she's trying to look out for me, but I just want to go with it. Let me make my mistakes and then afterwards just be there for me.

RICHARD: Right now, I work for Lake Shore Athletic Club, in the housekeeping department, but I'm getting ready to go back to school, maybe for an associate's degree. Housekeeping is the lowest of the low in the health club. We pick up towels. But as much as I get trashed on at work, I got to make sure my daughter has clothes, food, and everything she needs right now. Till I go to school and get something better I'm going to stay focused on keeping this job. Anyone can take the easy way out by hitting the streets and selling drugs, but I just need to make sure my daughter is straight. My mother always told me, "When you hang with the bad folks, you will be labeled as bad folks." I never got caught up in the drug thing. It's pretty much my mom saying, "Watch out what you do," and seeing things go down with my own eyes, that made me understand selling drugs is not the way to go.

VICTOR: I really don't have time to go out in the streets and get caught up in gang activity. My mother keeps me busy. She makes sure I am involved in extracurricular activities, and when they are over, she'll pick me up from school, so I don't really have the opportunity to loiter around and get myself into trouble. I don't think there is a single thing that my mother doesn't understand about me, because she has been through it herself. It may be a different time, but nothing has really changed. I know it hasn't been easy; it's nothing but hard work, but she is the best. If I tell my mother I love her every day, that really

means nothing unless I show her. That's why I try to make myself a model citizen, so people can say to my mother, "You've raised a great child." Every time someone tells her that, it makes her day, and it makes me happy.

RICHARD: I have made a promise to the mother of my child that I was never going to be like my father. I will never do what my father did to my mom. The way he just upped and left us, ass out. I told my mom that my daughter will be my number-one responsibility. I don't know what my mother planted in my head over the years, but I could have been just like a lot of people, "Oh forget it, I'm gone." The years of my mother talking to me drilled responsibility in my head, and it's sticking. I have to be there for my daughter. I want to be the same way for my daughter as my mother was for me and my brother. I'm just going to love my daughter as much as my mother loves me.

Sacred Bond

SCOTT CONOVER & SANDRA CONOVER

H A N D S - O N

Is a woman truly equipped to guide her son into manhood? Considering all the stories I heard from men who credit the influence of their mothers for their success, the answer is a resounding yes. Scott Conover is one of those men. He believes that his mother, Sandra Conover – a single mother, who depended on welfare at times – raised him to be a strong, responsible yet compassionate man. ■ His mother didn't like the idea of getting her picture taken. Unlike her son, she likes to stay on the sidelines – except when it comes to raising her children. She prides herself on not raising a typical professional football player. Conover, the first in his family to go to college, graduated with honors from Purdue University with a degree in industrial engineering. He was drafted right out of college as an offensive lineman for the Detroit Lions, but in his mother's opinion, his college degree still ranks number one among his accomplishments. ■ Inspired by his mother's devotion to her children, Conover has established the Scott Conover Youth Foundation, to give other children some of the opportunities his mother made possible for him. In Conover's life his mother has been everything to him: the father figure who taught him how to defend himself, the mother who feared for his safety, the mentor and coach who guided him toward the right decisions, and ultimately, the woman who taught her boy how to be a man.

SCOTT CONOVER
Professional Football Player
AGE TWENTY-EIGHT
MOTHER SANDRA CONOVER

When I was very young my legs were crooked and I had to wear corrective braces. My mother tells me that I always tried to keep up with the other kids but I just couldn't. It was a hard thing for her to see. After I got the braces removed I still had to practice walking straight, and other kids would tease me. She would tell me not to worry about the teasing: "You've got to stay focused on getting yourself better." She'd tell me that over and over again. I remember days when I was frustrated but she would push me to practice. "You're not doing it, you're not doing it," she'd say, and I would get even more frustrated. But she stayed on top of it to make sure I could walk straight. She was tough, but throughout my life she taught me how to be independent and responsible and how to fight back.

Even with seven children, my mother kept a close eye on us and was always there to make sure we stayed out of trouble. She also wanted to make sure we weren't taken advantage of. Older kids would pick on me a lot, and I was scared to fight back. Of course I'd come home crying to my mother. I remember she just said, "Don't let them hit on you. You are just as big as they are. Next time they hit you, you hit them back." Although she was never far behind, she made me go out there to face them. She expected me to stand up for myself, and after that the other kids stopped picking on me. I guess my mother knew that to be a strong black male you had to be able to fight. And that's what she taught me: to always fight for what you believe in and never give up. It has served me well out on the field; they hit and I hit them back.

A lot of the kids were afraid to come around. They'd say, "Man, your mother is mean." But it was really more tough than mean. She watched out for everybody and she was caring. It's hard to find parents now who will do that. When I was growing up everybody was like family and everybody watched out for each other. If another kid was getting in trouble my mother would let them know, "I know your mother and I'm gonna tell her what's going on."

My mother was definitely hands-on. She wanted us to do what was right. I remember one time when I was in third grade, I came home bragging that I got in a fight. But it was a fight with a little girl. I can remember the day so clearly. My mother took me and just swore me out. "You are a boy," she said. "You don't hit girls!" She would do whatever it took. If what we did was really bad, the punishment could be severe. It ranged from not being able to go out and play, to a spanking. Whatever it was, she was very firm.

But my mother always expressed love along with discipline. I can remember one day when I didn't take her seriously about something and she warned me, "You keep doing this, I'm gonna send you to bed without dinner." So I tried her, until one day she actually sent me to bed without supper. I thought she was playing around, but she was serious. I remember her waking me up in the middle of the night to tell me to come and get something to eat. She was just that kind of person, tough but compassionate. I didn't always understand while it was happening. I just thought my mother was over-protective. But looking back at it now, I'm glad. I can also see the difference between me and the other kids who had the freedom to do what they wanted. I can see how they ended up.

It was tough for my mother to raise seven children, but she managed to do whatever it took to keep us straight. There wasn't a lot of help for single mothers then. She really didn't have any time for herself. I never remember her going out to enjoy herself. She never went to any social events. She pretty much gave all of her time to her kids. She rarely spent money on herself; she spent it all on us. Any time we needed something,

she would do without. So when I say she did whatever it took, she pretty much took from herself to give to us.

We grew up in a small, three-bedroom home. My mother gave us the bedrooms and she slept on the couch or even on the floor, up to the time I went to college. I can remember coming home late at night seeing my mother sleeping there on the floor. It really bothered me. We didn't have a car, either; my mother walked wherever she had to go: to the store, to our school, even to work at the odds-and-ends jobs she had. It didn't make a difference if it was raining, snowing, or whatever, she had to walk home from work two miles every day, late at night by herself. I didn't think it was safe. I knew one day I would change that for her, and that really helped me stay focused. So the minute I graduated from college and went into the NFL, my first gift to my mother was a brand-new car. I surprised her with it on her birthday. Then the following

year I bought her a bigger house. Now we have a house with six bedrooms, and my mother finally has her own room. I made sure of that. I thought, whatever happens, you're gonna have your own room with your own bed. I just feel that I can never do enough to pay her back. I never get the feeling from her that I owe her anything; it's just the opposite – she is always saying, "You don't have to get me anything, save your money." But I always have to convince her, just like I had to convince her of me playing football.

For the longest time my mother didn't let me play football. She was afraid that I would get hurt, break my bones or something, because I was so skinny. She encouraged me to play other sports. Even when I graduated from college and got drafted by the Lions, she was saying, "Do you have to play football? You got your degree, you don't have to play anymore." Now that I play professional ball, she's starting to understand the game more. She even gets into it. She watches me on television, but she still covers her eyes when I'm out there hitting. I guess all mothers fear their children getting hurt. I know it was tough for her to see me get injured, but she has to understand that's the nature of the sport.

I've had three surgeries while playing for Detroit, a couple of knee surgeries and just recently one on my shoulder. My mother had never seen me injured, and I was never around her before during the healing process. But with this shoulder injury, she has been really involved. She has tried to baby me a little bit, like most mothers do. Because I've been away for so long I think she's trying to make up for that and try to do more things for me. This is the first time in ten or eleven years that I've spent a lot of time at home. I'm not used to it. I'm more independent, and I don't want to burden her.

My mother is still a strong woman, but I can tell a lot of her physical strength has weakened. It hurts to see that, because I realize how much time has passed – time I have missed with her. I remembered that before I left for college, she was still moving around furniture and refrigerators and stuff. I tell people all the time, my mother was strong back then; she could pick up a couch by herself. And I tell her she can't do that anymore. But my strength comes from hers.

I know how hard my mother worked trying to provide the best for us. I know the majority of her life wasn't easy, and that inspires me to move ahead and do my best. I will always have a piece of my mother in my heart, in all the things that she taught me. She was always there for me, and I know regardless of whatever happens in my life, she will always be there for me. I am fortunate that she cared enough to be tough, that she forced me to learn what was right. A lot of kids just don't have that.

LEWIS PAUL LONG & MARIE CLEMONS LONG SMITH

Although Lewis Paul Long's mother was not a single mother, she knew the importance of having not only one but several black male role models in her son's life. She wanted her son to benefit from the strengths of many. More so than any other mother I met, Marie Clemons Long Smith was intent on finding mentors for her son and ensuring that he learned from them. She also had those expectations of herself; she was just as intent on being a consistent mentor to her son. ■ When I met Long at the Old Executive Office Building in Washington, D.C., where he served as a White House Fellow, he showed me a folder filled with letters of inspiration that his mother had written to him over the years. She has remained to him a constant source of spiritual guidance and love. His mother is a teacher, and her dream for her son came true the day he visited her classroom to tell her that he had been accepted to Harvard Business School. Long is currently a senior adviser to the president of Howard University, where both he and his father are alumni. ■ Long's mother was the tie that bound the family together. She helped mend Long's fragile relationship with his father, Willie L. Long, and encouraged them to develop a mature relationship that has proved meaningful to them both. Ultimately, Long's story shows how crucial a mother can be in bolstering other significant relationships in her son's life.

LEWIS PAUL LONG
Business Executive
AGE THIRTY-ONE
MOTHER MARIE CLEMONS LONG SMITH

The summer of my sophomore year in college, my mother came to me and said, "Enough is enough. I've been with your dad for over twenty-five years, but I got to go." I said, fine, you need to get on with your life. I told her that leaving him was probably the best thing for everybody.

Over the years I had a lot of disappointment when it came to my father, but there is one incident that's been difficult to shake. It happened during my college graduation. We have the same birthday, and I graduated from Howard exactly twenty-five years to the day after he did. I felt that the graduation was something we should share despite the tension between us. He was always proud to be a Howard University graduate. So when I was graduating from his alma mater, I thought he would be really happy and proud about it, especially because I had done well.

At that time my parents' divorce proceedings were being finalized. My mom had sent him an announcement to my graduation, in spite of what was going on between them. She had also sent him newspaper articles about me because I had been accepted to Harvard Business School as a senior, which was pretty good. She was managing all of that for me. So the day of the graduation, I said to my father, "Where am I going to meet you?" He said, "I'm not going. You had your mother send that stuff to me and you didn't invite me personally." I told him mom took care of it because I was busy relocating, trying to find a job, an apartment. But he said, "No, I'm not coming." At that point I just shut down. It completely hurt me. Things like that created this arm's-length distance between us.

My mother never bad-mouthed my father. She encouraged our relationship from the moment she separated from him. She used to think that my father somehow felt that I had eclipsed his success, and that that may have created some feeling of envy. My mother tried to compensate for it, and she always pointed out my father's positive qualities. It was important to her that I have positive black male role models in my life, my father being the primary one. I also spent time with her brothers, who were educated and who had achieved a fair amount. And at church she always pointed out the deacons and black men who were elders. She also made sure that I spent summers with my grandfather, because he was such a strong figure in her life. I saw how he commanded respect in the largely segregated South of the early seventies, when most southern blacks didn't have anything.

My grandfather had a lot to do with my mother's strong-willed, independent nature. If there was something my mom wanted to happen, it would happen. My father called her Molly Brown, for the unsinkable ship. My mother always had her own bank account, would manage her own funds. It was very important to her to save her own money. I think her independence led my father to feel somewhat less than a husband. And for a long time I think he viewed me as my mother's child.

She was a great provider and is a good source of stability and spirituality in my life. She is always there to point out that life isn't as bad as it seems, or that things will always get better, or that I should go after whatever I want. However, I think for most of my life I have tried to contain my feelings for my mother. When I was seven, my mom was really ill. She was in the hospital for three weeks and the doctors didn't know what was wrong with her. They had no clue. She lost a lot of weight and got very weak. I remember her telling me, "Don't love me too much." Ever since, I've always felt like I had borrowed time. I was expecting to lose my mom, even though it was proven that she was better. Having lost her own mother at an early age, my mom kind of created some space, but there was definitely a lot of affection, a lot of love. My mom and I talk a fair amount, and if I don't talk to her, she will call and leave me

messages, usually words of inspiration. She's very spiritual, and I think that ties into her strength.

Within a short period of time after my mother and father divorced, she met this guy who had been widowed. He was also from the South, like my mom, and they had similar kinds of values and interests: first and foremost, church and God; and second, work and independence. They hit it off pretty well. I thought it was weird at first, because for so long my mother, sister, and I were our own clan. It was us against the world. And now there was this other person, who became a factor and knew all the intimate details and secrets of our life.

As things got more serious between them, my mother's biggest fear was that there might be contention between him and me. More than anything else, she wanted us to get along. She started bringing us together by introducing him to our Sunday-dinner ritual. He would come, and we would have open, frank

discussions. And if I had to have my car repaired or needed some advice, she'd say, "Why don't you call Al? He might be able to recommend a good mechanic." When I was buying my car, she suggested I talk to him. So we were able to build a substantive relationship, based on advice and guidance. He became kind of a father figure, supplementing what my own father might have been doing. It also gave him an opportunity to see that I was a pretty level-headed kid and had the same insecurities that any guy would have about someone dating his mother. I don't know if my mom was working on him the same way she was working on me, but it worked out. And I could tell he really cared for my mom. He came into her life at a time when my sister wasn't around and I felt like I wouldn't be around anymore. Their relationship relieved me of feeling obligated to stay, and allowed me to spread my wings.

During this time, my mother still encouraged me to visit my father and work on the relationship with him. She would always ask me, "How's your dad? Have you talked to him lately?" Once when I went to visit, I found him really sick, and I took him to the doctor. When he was in with the doctor the light came on. Right there he had congestive heart failure. They called the ambulance, put him on a stretcher, and rushed him to the hospital. I didn't know what to do. I just thought, "I can't believe this. All this time I've had this distant relationship with my father and now I'm going to end up being his caretaker." So the first thing I did was call my mother from the doctor's office. I told her what was happening. She told me, "This is what you have to do…. Ask these questions…." I was a little flipped out. I was thrust into the position of being the primary caretaker. I'm at the hospital and the doctors and nurses are asking about his next of kin, and it's me. My mother said, "Don't worry, it won't be a huge burden, and remember, he's your father."

I think that was a turning point in my relationship with my dad. I think he realized then, "I have this son and he's taking care of me." We never talk about events that occurred in the past; I'm sure he remembers, but now it doesn't matter anymore. Since the time I spent with him in the hospital, our relationship has grown stronger and we have developed a very solid relationship. We spent our last two birthdays together. He comes over to my house for dinner, I take him to the grocery store on Saturday mornings. Things have really changed, and I thank my mother for never allowing me to give up on him.

STUART SCOTT & JACQUELINE SCOTT

When he was growing up, Stuart Scott didn't have to look far for a positive male role model. His father, Orville Ray Scott Jr., was a strong patriarch who sometimes juggled two jobs at once and still was always there when his family needed him. His mother, Jacqueline Scott, wanted her son to be equally strong and self-assured. She didn't want him to be a caricature of what a man is "supposed" to be, as she had seen in others. Instead, she wanted all of her children to know that it was okay to be different. She armed each of them with the confidence to express their feelings and creativity, and that confidence has served Scott well in many areas of his life. ▪ An ESPN sportscaster, Scott spends most of his time in the rugged, aggressive world of sports. Yet Scott is not afraid to bring some uncharacteristic elements to the fray. His style of reporting includes a hip-hop flare that is considered radical in sports broadcasting. His mother doesn't understand his approach, but he credits her influence as the creative force behind his style. ▪ Scott's relationship with his mother has given him the freedom to express his individuality without fear or embarrassment. It allowed him to be as comfortable at a dance recital as he was at a football game. He is deeply grateful to his mother for nurturing the confidence that allows him to be on the cutting edge and the sensitivity that has made him a better husband and father. Simply put, his mother's influence has made him a better man.

STUART SCOTT
ESPN Sportscaster
AGE THIRTY-THREE
MOTHER JACQUELINE SCOTT

I have found that I am able to talk about my feelings better than a lot of men. With my wife, I am always saying, Kim, tell me what you feel, or, why do you feel like this? or, I feel this because....I got that from my mother, who was always very open with me about how she felt. She didn't raise me to believe that it's not cool for a man to say I love you or I care about you. She raised me to express my emotions.

From the time I was about a year old, whenever the song "Edelweiss" from *The Sound of Music* came on, my mother would pick me up and dance with me. The movie usually ran on television once a year, and even as I got older, whenever the song came on my mom and I would hug. Now whenever I hear the song, I pick up my daughter and we dance. Then I call my mother to let her know it's on. She tears up. It's just a thing we share.

My mother exposed us to a lot of different things, all kinds of diverse music, plays, and musicals. My parents would take my brother and sisters and me on different kinds of family outings. I love musicals now because we grew up doing our chores every Saturday listening to music from *West Side Story*, *Jesus Christ Superstar*, *Camelot*, *Godspell*, and *The Sound of Music*. She also introduced us to all kinds of things that weren't necessarily considered cool for a black kid to do.

When we moved from an all black neighborhood in Chicago to a white neighborhood in North Carolina, we were the first black everything: the first black family on the block, the first blacks playing in Little League baseball and football, the first black everything. We didn't have lots of conversations about it and I don't think my mother spent much time saying, you're black so it's going to be hard for you. But she did little things to give us confidence. I remember whenever she would give us a birthday card she would color the faces brown and draw them with curly hair. At Christmas she once took shoe polish and made the angel on top of the tree black. That might not be anything special now, but it was back then. She concentrated on giving us a positive self-image. She concentrated on letting us know that we were good kids and we could achieve whatever was before us.

Mom was zipping around Winston-Salem constantly. She took us everywhere. My dad was working two jobs, one at the post office and another at ADT security. Almost every night she'd take him dinner or pick him up from the job at midnight. She'd get the four of us out of bed, bundle us up, and drive to wherever my father was. As we got older, my brother, one of my sisters, and I were playing sports, and the other sister was in cheerleading and the dancing boots, so my mother was taking us to this Little League baseball game here, a high school basketball game there, dancing-boots practice. She was a teacher's aide, so she didn't get off work till four or five o'clock, but as a kid, you think this is no big deal — I got to go here, so Mom's going to take me. But then you grow up and you get married and you have a child of your own, and you wonder, how did she do it all? How did she do it with four kids? Now I realize the sacrifices it required.

I think my mother grew up seeing that kind of sacrifice. She was the second oldest of four children. Her father was mugged in the streets of Chicago, shot and killed when she was only six years old. Her mother never remarried, and my mother watched her raise four kids by herself. So she knew about sacrifice. But unlike her mother, she had my father's support. This year my mother and father hit forty years of marriage.

I think my father was much more hands-on than other fathers of his generation. He worked two or three jobs and then finally got a postal inspector job, but he always worked a lot of hours. My brother and I marvel about this: whenever we asked Dad to come out and throw a football with us, we can only remember one time when he said, "I can't, I'm too tired."

And that one time, ten minutes later he came out anyway. Whenever we were outside throwing a ball, my mother would come out and want to play with us. When we were playing football with the other little boys, she would come and want to kick the ball. She never wanted to throw it, she would kick it. She was the only mom in the neighborhood who did that.

I think as a child the best thing was to be scared of getting in trouble. And I definitely was. I could count the times my mother was angry on one hand. If she let a curse word slip we knew, uh-oh, Mom's mad. My mother was a disciplinarian, a little easier than my dad, but I didn't like getting in trouble with her. And I didn't like the spankings. Some mothers used belts or paddles, but my mom used one of those thick blue cords from an old iron to spank us. We used to hide that thing because we didn't want to get spanked. When all of us were older we had a ceremonial burying of that ironing cord.

People talk about how there shouldn't be any corporal punishment, how you shouldn't spank your kids. What I say to that is, I got spanked and I turned out all right. Parents always say this hurts me more than it hurts you. My mother said that, and I used to think, no it doesn't. But now that have a child of my own, it's true. I have to spank my daughter from time to time. I hate doing it and I wish I could just let her do whatever she wants, but I can't.

My relationship with my mom has been consistently good, and I think part of the reason why is that we're able to talk about the things that hurt us or the things that bugged me. My mother never hesitated to say, Stuart, I don't like it when you do that, or, Stuart, you don't need to do this. She is the most honest person I know. It's almost a joke now how she parents all the time. I tell her sometimes, "Mom, just be my friend."

"Well, I'm going to be your mother," she says.

My mother doesn't always understand everything I do. She said to me once, "Why do you have to use all of this hip-hop stuff when you do your sportscast?" She just doesn't get into the whole hip-hop scene and doesn't understand half the things I'm using. She also doesn't realize that the reason I am secure in bringing hip-hop to sports is because she raised me to be unique. It was cool to be a football player and then to put on some leg warmers and go be in a theater production. It was cool to play tennis and run track and also act. It was cool for my mother to send me as a young black man off on a skiing trip. Because of my mother, I felt like no matter what I do, it's okay to be different. There were no stereotypes in our house. There were no directives saying this is how you have to be. I was a black kid growing up listening to *The Sound of Music.* And there isn't much difference between that and being a sportscaster and using hip-hop. It is easy for me to be comfortable with it, because that is how my mother raised me.

179

Before Randall Robinson would agree to be interviewed for this book, he wanted to know if its focus was only on single mothers. He didn't want to help perpetuate any negative stereotype of fatherless black families. Robinson himself was raised in a household with a strong patriarch, Maxie Robinson Sr., and with a mother, Doris Robinson Griffin, who played an important supporting role. Only as an adult did Robinson begin to see his mother as the powerful independent force she is, a woman with a commitment to service much like his own. ▪ Robinson is the founder and president of TransAfrica, a foreign policy lobbying organization that helped launch democracy in South Africa and restore it in Haiti. He has an unwavering commitment to people of color around the world and to making issues that affect them an integral part of the American agenda. Robinson's parents cultivated his penchant for strong political stands. They taught him, his late brother, and his two sisters to be uncompromising in their beliefs, and the result was four extraordinarily independent minded children: a human rights activist, the first black network television news anchor, an actress, and a soon-to-be minister. ▪ A steady and constant presence in his life, Robinson's mother always exhibited a quiet strength. During times when eyes all over America were focused on her two sons, she didn't buckle under public pressure or innuendo. She has guided her family through some difficult times, steadfastly encouraging them to stand their ground.

RANDALL ROBINSON
President, TransAfrica
AGE FIFTY-SIX
MOTHER DORIS ROBINSON GRIFFIN

I had to grow up a bit to appreciate my mother's kind of strength. My father was a proud and principled man, one of enormous muscular carriage. When I was a child I was frightened by his size, but he was always fair, a benevolent despotic guy in the mold of fathers of that era. The girls didn't get whippings, but my brother, Max, and I got some very memorable ones, which we deserved. My father taught history and coached all of the sports at the high school we attended. He coached me in basketball. I always thought that Daddy was the pillar of strength in the family, and he definitely was, but my mother's strength was as great if not greater than his. It was less visible but certainly just as tough.

So much of my mother's life was lived in poverty and in segregation. She had no career. She stayed at home as a homemaker and spent her time with us. She has never complained, although I'm sure she's got things about which to complain. But her attitude would be, what's the value of complaining, and why burden anyone else with it? I suppose the decision to stay home and take care of the family was a difficult one, because she was a brilliant woman. Now that I look back on it, it was a choice made at quite a price. There is no question that if my mother were graduating from college now, she'd become a hugely successful professional woman.

It was only after my father died that she learned to drive, when she was sixty. She got her license, bought a car, got a job. She became the executive director of the Richmond YWCA after forty years or so of not working, after raising four children, after her marriage. My mother is now eighty-four and still strong. She still drives, still gardens; her mind is as clear as could be. You don't have to be around her long to know how whole and impressive she is: she insists on living alone in her own house, going to church on Sunday, cooking her own meals, gardening, driving her own car, going down on occasion to the Outer Banks with her friends, and traveling around the country making speeches. She's a hugely secure person. And in her own way, she has always known how to accomplish what she's set out to accomplish.

Both of my parents felt strongly that it's what you believed in that counted, and no matter how many people stood against it, if you thought it was right you stayed the course and stood your ground. Both Momma and Daddy encouraged that kind of independence of spirit and enterprise. They were not cookie-cutter people, and I think that has a lot to do with how we were reared. There were four children; one became a network news anchor, another became a foreign policy person, another is acting, and another at age fifty is in divinity school.

My mother had broadly defined ambitions for her children. She wanted us to be good people. She would say, I want you to be prepared for life, I want you to get a good education, I want you to work hard, I want you to uphold your obligations and responsibilities as mothers and fathers, and, I want you to be good, decent human beings. She never said, I want you to be a doctor, or, I want you to be a lawyer. It was never prescriptive in that way. We all were given a wide berth to choose what we wanted to do, even if it took some of us, especially me, and to some extent Max, a while to discover what we wanted to do. But never did she try to dictate, even where we wanted to go to college. She would give advice, but it was never heavy-handed. I think we felt pressure to do well, but not pressure to do this or that. We never felt her trying to live through us. She loved her children, but she knew that they were whole, grown, independent people, who were able to determine their course largely because of the equipment their parents had given them. I think she also believed she had responsible children. We never caused her a great deal of worry and heartache.

She wanted us to live, and she was in her own right an important force in her home, in her community, in her world.

When I went on the hunger fast for Haiti, I told my mother what I was going to do and why I was doing it. She said she would pray for me and that she knew I was doing it for the right reasons and was proud of me. She never told me not to do it, never burdened me with that kind of thing. She understood that life is fraught with risk. Of course my mother was worried about what I was doing, especially because she wasn't there with me. She was in Norfolk, and I would talk to her regularly and tell her what the doctor was doing and what kind of state I was in. Somewhere around day 25 of the strike I had to be hospitalized for dehydration. They ran a picture in *USA Today*, and it made me look like I was at death's door. I think that scared her. She was greatly relieved when it ended. During the course of the hunger strike somebody actually said to her,

"You've lost one son and now you're losing the other." They were talking about my brother, Maxie.

When he got sick he was in Chicago with ABC News. I was here in Washington, and Mama was in Norfolk. We had talked a lot to him on the phone, and he seemed to be getting sick a lot. He didn't know what was going on, he just complained about flu-like symptoms. We hadn't seen him in a few months, so we didn't know. I was married in June of '87 at Mama's house by my stepfather. My son was my best man, and of course my brother came. Max was six two and normally weighed about 215. He was markedly thinner when he arrived for the wedding.

We got a call in early December from a friend in Chicago, saying Max was in the hospital and they didn't know what was going on. He said the doctors were doing all kinds of tests. They didn't find anything, and finally decided to test him for AIDS. He just didn't fit the profile then of someone who would come down with AIDS. I don't think he thought about it as a possibility, and if he did he certainly hadn't shared it with us. At first the test came back negative, so we breathed a sigh of relief. Then, two or three days later, the doctor called back and said they had done another AIDS test and it was positive.

We all had a very hard time with that, and Mama was greatly grieved. But she is naturally a strong person; she handles everything with great strength. My mother didn't care what people thought about my brother having AIDS. We didn't care. I've never even discussed it, never thought about what the public thought. Our mother didn't raise her family to care about what the public thinks. She raised us to care about what we think of ourselves.

During Max's illness we became a closer family than we had been perhaps for many years. And in many ways it was Max's finest hour. He demonstrated a brand of courage I had not seen from him before, a brand of courage of which to this day I'm not sure I would be capable. He drew us to him and released us to love him and love each other. Through it all Mama did not seek anyone's pity, she did not lean on anyone. Her son, Max, died at Howard University Hospital at the end of the following year, 1988.

You never get over it. I think of Max every day, and I'm sure Mama does. I don't think my relationship with my mother changed after Max died. I don't think she was any more concerned or afraid about what I was doing. I think the most terrifying thing for me would be to die before she does, because I know it would just tear her apart. It's terribly difficult for a mother to see her child die. No parent is really prepared for that. I just hope, God, please let my mother go before me.

CARL JEFFREY WRIGHT & LOTTIE MAE THOMAS WRIGHT

THE WOMAN OF THE HOUSE

The men I talked with who were raised by both parents seemed to share one thing in particular: many of them didn't fully recognize their mother's personal strength until much later in life. Carl Jeffrey Wright, like several men I interviewed, didn't fully understand the magnitude of his mother's accomplishments until he was well established as an adult with his own family. ▪ The interesting thing is, to most people his mother's strength was patently obvious: Lottie Mae Wright raised seven boys, went back to school at the same time, and went on to a successful twenty-year career as a librarian. She ran the central library system in Washington, D.C., and later accepted a similar position at a nearby university. She did all of this with only one arm and one leg, yet her disability was never an issue in her family. She took it for granted, and so, naturally, did her children. ▪ Wright's mother never used the circumstances of her life as an excuse, and she expected the same from her sons. Wright is now the president of Urban Ministries, Inc., a twenty-eight-year-old African American–owned and –operated Christian publishing company. He earned his law degree from Georgetown University and a master's in business administration from Columbia University. ▪ During a recent personal crisis, Wright was reminded of the depth of his mother's commitment and her extraordinary capability. Their story is a striking example of how a mother's strength – if you're lucky – is something you can depend on for life.

CARL JEFFREY WRIGHT
Publisher
AGE FORTY-THREE
MOTHER LOTTIE MAE THOMAS WRIGHT

My parents had a strong, very stable relationship until my father passed away, in April of '93. They had been married for fifty-two years and had seven sons, no daughters. My mother was the only woman in a household of eight men, but she wasn't swallowed up. No way. A lot of things that happened in our house happened at her command, and you had to do it her way. And if you didn't, her husband would get you. My dad had the attitude, this is my wife, you got to deal with her not just as your mom but as the person who is special to me. And he treated her like royalty. My father had the primary responsibility for cooking for the family. My mother ate one thing, we ate different stuff. Her status was special. If my mom was out of town it was not unusual for my dad to undertake a major project to surprise her when she came home, like the kitchen being painted or something in the yard improved. It was the idea that the most significant thing you can do is something to make your mom happy.

I suppose my father was so accommodating to my mother because of her physical limitation. When my mother was eight, she was run over by a train. She lost her left arm below the elbow and her left leg. I was about eight before I even noticed. My mother did everything, she sewed, she cooked. She didn't drive; in fact, neither my mother nor my father drove. The only thing I can ever remember doing for her specifically because of her handicap was thread a needle. She could sew with one arm, but you needed two hands to thread a needle.

It hit me that my mother had a disability one day when we were at the laundromat. We didn't have a washer and a dryer growing up. So one of the rituals of my childhood was getting our clothes, putting them in one of those little wire carts, and going around the corner to the laundromat. On this occasion, my younger brother and I were with my mother, and I was putting clothes in the dryer. An attendant, an old white woman, comes over to me and says: "Is that your mother over there with the — " and she does this chopping motion on her left arm. Then it hit me, my mother only has one arm. It kind of blew me away, because my mother was so independent. I see plenty of people in wheelchairs who have less physically wrong with them than my mom, yet she was never in a wheelchair. The word "handicap" was never used in my household. The only time anything ever came up that I can remember is every few years or so my mother would go to get her prosthetic leg adjusted. She also had a prosthetic arm. I remember one of my brothers finding the arm in a closet one day. "Hey, there's this arm up there," he said. "That's Mom's arm," we told him, but she never wore it, because at that time prosthetic arms weren't at all functional.

One time when we were kids, we were arguing over something with one of our neighbors. Back in the sixties the worst thing you could say to someone else was "Your mother." Well, that's all this neighbor had to say to get things going, but he took it even further. During this fight he said to my older brother, who was always the biggest, "Your peg-legged mother." I was like, whoa. Well, after Johnny finished demolishing his butt, I thought he didn't just say "your mother," but he made something of the fact that my mother had just one leg. That's probably the most devastating fight I can ever remember from childhood, watching my older brother react to this guy for criticizing my mother's handicap. But the handicap in no way compromised her perception of herself or how we perceived her.

I don't think she was any harder on us because of what she was able to overcome. I think the way she raised us was the way she would have raised us regardless of the disability. Now, you can't separate a person from the major crises of their life, so it probably wouldn't be correct to say that her disability didn't influence her feelings about success and personal determination. But it's not like she ever said, if I can do it, you can do it, or, I clean house with one arm, so therefore you ought to be able to clean it twice as fast. It was nothing like that. She just did it. And you just went forward because she said go forward.

As I got older I would think back to my mom and what she was able to accomplish. I can recall a period when I lived in New York, it was not unusual to see a person with one leg sitting in a wheelchair holding a cup of pencils. You got to be kidding, I'd just laugh to myself. What's your problem? You got two arms and your only problem is one leg is gone and you think you should be begging.

I had this very clear picture of the strength of human will, and I think my mother gave me what somebody might call a success imprint, that there's this level of achievement that has to be possible because of what you saw in your own household.

What some people would view as an impossibility, you just take for granted. I'm sure this came through osmosis, from watching my mom succeed. I saw a woman who grew up in a poor preacher's family in the South, one of eleven kids, finish college and graduate. And by the way, she had one arm, one leg, and seven sons and was able to become very successful in her field. I saw my mom do anything, so I knew I could do anything.

This last year in particular, I've been reintroduced to my mother. I got divorced and received custody of my three children, and my mother spent the year with me, helping me with my children. It was a messy divorce. Even though I got custody, my ex-wife didn't leave our residence. It was horrible for the kids. I asked my mother to come, initially at the prodding of my lawyer. I was at risk of my ex-wife provoking an incident, feigning abuse, or something else that could have resulted in getting me kicked out of the house and separated from my children.

The first time I asked my mother to come she said, "It's not as serious as you think."

"No, it really is," I told her, but she said no anyway. The next time I called her it was different.

"Mama, I need you," I said. She heard the urgency in my voice and she came. So my mother became my live-in witness as well as a caretaker for the kids.

My mother was always that way; she would drop whatever, if one of us guys needed her. She was extremely responsive. It's hard to imagine how you could get everything you want from someone with so many kids, but you did with my mother. Whoever had the need, she met that need. It's still true to this day. Before I spent this time being mothered again, I didn't really appreciate my mother like I do now. She is the anchor of my character. Seeing her commitment to me during the last year, I realize nobody else in the world would do that.

I suppose lots of people say, my mom has always been there for me, but to see that in a real way as an adult, I believe I've been uniquely blessed. My mother coming through for me in what looked like a life-or-death situation, well, I needed my mother as an adult and she came even though she was seventy-six years old and handicapped. She was able to bring something only a mother could. Your wife will divorce you, I can tell you that, but your mother will love you no matter what.

After this experience of "adult mothering," I understood a little bit better my dad's caretaking of my mother. It wasn't because of her disability after all. I'd say that if my dad took extra special care of my mom, it was because that's how he felt about her, period. He simply loved his wife for the incredible woman that she is.

ROCK NEWMAN & SARAH GERTRUDE NEWMAN

THE ROCK

There never was a time when Eugene "Rock" Newman could ignore his mother's influence on her family — it's simply too powerful. The oldest mother in this collection of interviews, Sarah Gertrude Newman has nurtured five generations of Newmans and has been a rock not only for her family but for an entire community. Everybody in Brandywine, Maryland, knows and relies on "Gertie." The security she represents allowed her son to venture out and make his fortune in the high-stakes, high-risk world of professional boxing. ■ Newman has enjoyed enormous success as a boxing promoter and manager. He guided the careers of heavyweight champions Michael Spinks and Riddick Bowe. One of his greatest coups, however, was in the political arena. Newman has been credited for single-handedly orchestrating the comeback of Washington, D.C., mayor Marion Barry after his drug conviction and incarceration. Newman's career has not escaped public criticism, but the judgment of only one person — his mother — really matters to him. ■ While Newman and his mother were being photographed, one of his sisters said to me, "We are all her children, but Rock is her baby." She was commenting on the special relationship that Newman and their mother share. Through the years his sister has seen how Gertrude Newman has been a stabilizing force in her last-born child's life, and how he in turn has provided security in hers. Their story shows how a great matriarch can inspire many generations and provide a much-needed anchor for her son.

ROCK NEWMAN
Boxing Promoter
AGE FORTY-FIVE
MOTHER SARAH GERTRUDE NEWMAN

When I told my mother I was leaving a secure job at Howard University to do this boxing thing full time, she was very concerned. "Boy, you are crazy," she said. "Give up your regular paycheck?" This whole thing about business and boxing and the people you had to deal with made her afraid. Her greatest fear was that I would go broke, that I wouldn't be able to feed myself without a weekly check coming in, even though I only started out making a little more than $14,000 a year at Howard. And I don't even know what she imagined about the "boxing people."

I have never wanted to do anything to violate my mother's sense of decency. I don't have a halo on my head, but part of what keeps me in a zone of respectability, even in the boxing world, is trying not to disappoint my mother. That's part of what keeps me in line. The sense of security she provides is where I draw my strength to be a risk-taker, and I've taken some very serious risks in my life. I operate on the understanding that if the rest of the world thinks I'm a fool or a failure, or even worse, that's not what my mother would think. So if I took a risk and fell and ever had to go back to Brandywine, Maryland, to my childhood home, it would be like nothing ever happened at all.

Brandywine is a rural community. Everybody there knows my mother as Miss Gertie, Aunt Gertie, or Grandma Gertie. She is ninety years old now and a very tiny lady. For sixty years my mother has lived in the same house. It's a very small house. My mother and father raised all of us there, my five brothers, two sisters, and me. We didn't have indoor plumbing until I was about sixteen. But even though the house is slight, it is still a hub of activity for the community. Cousins, neighbors, friends, or whoever used to come over to our place. My mother was always like, just go in the refrigerator and pour some tea, make yourself a balogna sandwich. Or she would make it for you. It was like that and still is. A few years ago I tried to buy my mother a new house. You know how we do, when we get some money, we gonna buy Mama a house. But my mother has absolutely resisted.

"I don't care what you say," she said to me, "I'm not gonna leave my house. I don't care if you built me a mansion, it wouldn't be home." So I've paved the driveway, put up aluminum siding, built a porch, and done the cabinets. She's cool with that kind of stuff.

Everybody, the children, the grandchildren, the great-grandchildren, and even some great-great-grandchildren, see my mother as a source of strength, as the glue that keeps the family together. *She* probably should have been named Rock. I never put it that way before in my life. But that's what she was: a rock, strong and always there for everybody. She's the one who cooked, literally, three meals a day. Every single day – three cooked meals! She washed, she ironed. I didn't think anything of it at the time, but that's what she did for her family. She had a reservoir to give. And the interesting thing is, it remains so today. A couple of my nephews who are in their thirties have had drug problems. My mother is their connection to sanity. I got each of them into an excellent drug program, and they say that their inspiration to get better is Grandma Gertie. Even the counselors and the guy who runs the place said, "I don't know you ma, but if it wasn't for her, these guys might not have what they needed to fight this battle."

I think that inspiration comes from her unconditional love. There's some sense that she's the anchor, and before you're gonna go over the edge she'll be there to hook you. And I'm not talking about ten years ago, when she was eighty. It's right now. We are not a terribly verbal family. We weren't the kind of family that said I love you and all that. There was so

much more than the words; there was an incredible example of that love right before us.

My dad was a cement-truck driver. He had diabetes and had to retire from his job when I was twelve. For some reason he couldn't get Social Security or any retirement benefits for close to a year and a half. My mother managed somehow without any money coming in, to keep things going. There was obviously some "little savings" somewhere, and during that time we never missed a meal. One of my older brothers would come by and say, "Mom, are you sure you don't want something?"

"No, maybe in a couple months I might have to borrow something," she'd answer. But never did. She wouldn't take anything from anybody.

We would definitely be characterized as poor. My mother still doesn't talk about it to me much, but she tells my wife, Dee Dee, about the times when she would go for two weeks without any money. Not a penny. It

seems inconceivable to me, because she never let us know, and also because she would always loan other people money. I thought we were rich. And it's interesting, because I got a lot of things that my older sisters and brothers didn't get, because of the twelve-year difference. My brothers and sisters caught hell. They were sleeping three to a bed and wearing hand-me-downs. I got first runs all the way. My mother wanted me to have the best.

My mother was embarrassed when she found out she was pregnant with me. She told the doctor, "I cannot be pregnant. I'm almost forty-six years old. You have made a mistake." Well, it wasn't a mistake. My father was, like, beating his chest. The doctor who delivered me told my mother that a baby born on a change of life was going to be a smart baby. I don't know whether this played a part in my mother's expectations of me. I don't think she necessarily had high social expectations, and I can't say there was any great thrust toward higher education, because my mother only had an eighth-grade education. I think my dad had a sixth-grade education. There had been no one really in my family to achieve anything of any substance. My mother just wanted us to be good, to behave ourselves. She didn't want us to embarrass ourselves or the family.

Probably the biggest conflict my mother and I had growing up was my choice of girlfriends. For some reason, I was drawn to the blackest little girls you could find. My mother had this issue of color, as do many African American families. My mother wasn't enlightened yet. I say "yet," because she's a down sister now. Color doesn't matter anymore. But aside from the color issue, my mother thought that I was associating with girls who were from families who had some problems. I think she was petrified that I would fall into the "wrong hands" and would be

led astray. I never based who I went out with on my mother's approval. I probably had enough machismo to say that it didn't matter what my mother thought about that. But somewhere in there, when she did approve, I had a measure of comfort. I never really looked for anyone like my mother, but I wanted someone who would bring the sense of stability my mother had. I wanted an anchor, because I didn't see myself being one. I was always out there doing something.

When I was thirty-one and getting ready to get married, something seemed to make my mother feel as if she were losing me. Dee Dee and I had already announced we were getting married. So we went down to Brandywine to visit my mother one day. We walked in the house just kind of playing, and my wife said, "Rock and I have decided that we are not going to get married." She wasn't ready for my mother's response.

"Oh, that's the best news I've heard in my life," my mother said.

Dee Dee was messed up. When we left the house I saw it all over her. So I stopped the car at a Safeway and called my mother. I said, "Now, I am going to marry her. If you feel bad, I'm sorry. But I'm a man and this is a decision I have made. I also want you to know that if you think you are going to lose me because I am getting married, that's not the case."

"I was only kidding," she said. But I knew it was more than that. It was probably the moment. My mother and Dee Dee love each other to death. Dee Dee tells her how who I am and what I've become is an extension of her. I don't know if she ever really thinks of herself in that way. My mother is so humble and takes nothing for granted. She has an innate kind of humility and doesn't really recognize how significant she has been in my life. But if I say my mother means everything to me, that's still not enough. She is my conscience. She's my guardian angel.

I talk to my mother every day to just find out what's going on. There are days I might talk to her two or three times, no matter where I am. When I call her from another country she is always amazed. "Where are you calling from?" she'll ask, and I'll tell her where. "God, I can't believe you're all the way there. When you gonna slow down?" She never knows what to expect. I had a dinner recently and the whole thing cost maybe ten grand. She couldn't believe it. "I can't see how in the world you spend that kind of money," she said. "You going to be broke and cause me to lose my check from coming in." Later she said to me, "I was talking to Edna, and I told her that if I'd known I was gonna get all this, I'd have had you a lot earlier so I could enjoy it when I was younger." My mother often says how she feels by saying what she was telling somebody else. She tells Edna she is proud of me – but still worries that I'll fall.

Sacred Bond

STEPHEN LEONARD & BEATRICE LEONARD

Stephen Leonard's mother is also a strong matriarch — one who didn't spare the rod. In an era when corporal punishment is frowned on, almost everyone I interviewed had at least one story about what playwright George C. Wolfe calls "black mama whippings." These are old-fashioned spankings that in practice range from a slap on the butt to what now would be considered child abuse. Many of the men, in retrospect, actually thank their mothers for keeping them in line. Yet no one spoke more fondly of his whippings, or was more appreciative of his mother's discipline, than Stephen Leonard. He felt that his mother's actions have made the critical difference between his success and failure in life.
■ Supported by a hardworking husband, Beatrice Leonard raised a family with wholesome values and morals. Over the years, Leonard has taken some heat from his friends about the way he was raised. His family has been called everything from the "Brady Bunch" to the *"Redbook* family." To Leonard, though, his family's wholesomeness is his badge of honor. ■ Leonard grew up to be what most American boys used to dream of being: a sergeant in the fire department. In his work, he often sees the consequences of parental neglect, and he knows the importance of a mother's watchful eye. Leonard's relationship with his mother is a testament to how the right combination of discipline, involvement, and love can steer a child toward a rich and productive life — the ultimate American dream.

STEPHEN LEONARD
Firefighter
AGE THIRTY-SIX
MOTHER BEATRICE LEONARD

I grew up in what is probably considered a lower-middle-class neighborhood in Maryland, just outside of Washington, D.C. Our house was on a horseshoe-shaped block, and the entire block had the same type of semidetached houses all the way around. In the neighborhood there were maybe twenty or thirty guys around my age, and only two or three of us didn't go to jail. I'm talking about a group of guys coming from the same background with pretty much the same type of family setup. I really believe the difference was our mothers. A lot of kids on my block had discipline to a certain degree, but their mothers didn't have the same involvement in their children's lives that my parents did. My mother knew exactly how she wanted to raise her kids. She knew exactly what path she wanted for them: she wanted all of us to go to college. She impressed that on us at an early age and never compromised.

My mother was a stern disciplinarian and so was my father, but usually at her beckoning. If we did something, she'd give us our punishment and add, "When your father gets home, he's going to punish you too." My brother and I talk about this all the time. I think he might have gotten one spanking in his life, but I used to get spanked, like, every other day, because I was always doing something. I was the oldest, and I think it was my mother's mission in life to make an example out of me for my brother and sister. I wanted to be outside all the time, so my mother knew that to keep me in line, all she had to do was say, "You have to stay in the house." I could take twenty spankings instead of one day in the house.

Dinnertime was important to my family. I think that was more of my mother's doing than my father's. It was very important to her that the whole family sit down and eat together every day. She always cooked. My sister always helped clean up. My brother and I would help sometimes, but not often. We had other chores to do. After dinner my father would leave to drive a cab or go to one of his other jobs.

But I think eating dinner together kept my family close because we would talk about what happened during the day. It was a time to share back and forth. I think that's what made our family different than the other kids'. I didn't know there was any other way to have dinner until my early teens when I went to my friend's house on the block. He would come in to eat whenever he felt like it. His mother would cook and leave food on the stove. A couple of other friends had it worse. They would pretty much find something in the refrigerator and make their own dinner. I thought everyone ate like we did, but now I know I was fortunate.

My mother was involved in our lives from sunup to sundown. She worked as a secretary at the elementary school that we all went to. It was good, because all of the teachers knew me. I would be one of the first kids to go on the great trips and stuff like that. But it was also bad, because I was always getting into something and my mother was always the first to find out. She handled discipline problems and anything that came up until the principal could get there. So to me, my mother was the principal of the school. I remember there was a "bad table" in the cafeteria for the kids who did something wrong. This table was directly across the hall from the principal's office. One time I was sitting at the bad table, hunching over my lunch bag, trying not to be seen. When I looked up, my mother was standing across the counter in the office. I could see her face, her eyes just glaring at me. "Oh God," I thought. When the bell rang, my mother just looked at me and waved her finger to come here. I walked in the office and she asked me what I did. I can't even remember; it was something minor like talking back to a teacher. But I do remember that she said, "When you get home, I'm going to straighten this out." That's all she needed to say.

I went back to my class, and all day long I was worried about what would happen when I got home. By the time I got there she had already talked to the teacher and basically had the story. "Take your schoolbooks with you and go to your room," she ordered. "And don't come downstairs until dinnertime." You knew not to defy her because the retribution would be swift and severe.

In some instances she used a paddle, a little paddle we got from one of those little theme parks around here. Written on the paddle was "Heat for the seat." It had a little boy with long-john underwear on, the red union suit, with his butt out and lightning bolts coming off it. I remember I got an Unsatisfactory in behavior in the second grade. The paddle and I were good friends that summer. My mother talked to me first about why I got the Unsatisfactory. I tried to explain to her why in my little kiddie way, but I knew it was just me. And then she spanked me

203

with that paddle and said, "You're going to stay in the house until school starts next year. The whole summer." Then she said, "When your father gets home, he's going to spank you." And sure enough, when my father came home, he pulled a belt out of his pants. But guess what, I never got another U in behavior.

I think her daily involvement with us kept us from even thinking about doing the things that most kids think about doing. I saw kids trying drugs and I saw kids shoplifting candy and the works. My mother knew just about everything we did and didn't do. She knew the people we played with, she knew the kid around the corner who was a troublemaker, the one who got kicked out of school or was brought down to the office five or six days out of a month. She knew what happened before we did. She wouldn't let us go to just anybody's house. "I don't want you going around so-and-so's house," she'd warn us. "He is going nowhere fast." There was a joke around the neighborhood: "If Miss Leonard doesn't know about it, then it didn't happen." She knew everything that went on, and the kids in the neighborhood knew she would tell. So they wouldn't do too much around her. It wasn't that they were afraid of my mother, I think it was more that they were respectful.

My mom is one of my best friends. I can truly say, that out of all the friends I have, and I believe I have a lot of close friends, when I get really down about something I don't call one of my boys, because a lot of times they're going to joke and dismiss you. And I hate to say it, but I don't call my wife, I call my mother. I don't want to sound like some kind of psycho or something, that I don't love and care for my wife. On a day-to-day basis, my wife and my child are first. I try to get my wife to understand that, but when I get that call from my mother and she needs me, barring a flood or something, I'm going to help her. Sometimes I feel my wife doesn't understand, especially when there are things to do around our own house. The first thing in my wife's mind is to quote from the Bible: "Cleave unto your wife." And she's right. I found that, in marriage, the best thing to do is find a middle ground, and I think I have been successful at it. But there is no middle ground when it comes to my mother. She was always there for me. I can't even fathom the idea of saying no to her.

TABB BISHOP & THE REVEREND LOUISE WILLIAMS BISHOP

EYES WATCHING OVER YOU

Tabb Bishop's mother was omnipotent in her children's lives – but in a way very different from that of Stephen Leonard's mother. The Reverend Louise Williams Bishop is a highly visible woman in Philadelphia, and when her children were growing up she literally had eyes all over the city looking out for them. Because of this there wasn't too much that Bishop, his two brothers, and his sister could do without their mother finding out about it. Few other children received a comparable level of public support (and public scrutiny). ■ Not only is Bishop's mother a minister, she is also a radio personality and a politician. His mother's career has been a source of inspiration to Bishop; after helping his mother win a seat in the Pennsylvania General Assembly, he got involved in politics himself. Bishop is now a lobbyist, representing such concerns as public education and economic development in Philadelphia. He is also enrolled in divinity school to become a minister like his mother. ■ Unlike many women, Reverend Bishop was blessed with an unusually broad base of support. When she became a single working mother, she could reach out to the community of people she had been contributing to for many years. Tabb Bishop is a beneficiary of a community at work – on a large scale. This mother-son relationship gives new meaning to the phrase "It takes a village," and Bishop says he doesn't know what he would have become without it.

TABB BISHOP
Lobbyist
AGE THIRTY-TWO
MOTHER THE REVEREND
LOUISE WILLIAMS BISHOP

———

I can remember that back in my college days when people used to hang out all night, my mother was still trying to have me back by midnight. One night I was out having a real good time at a house party. Everybody was dancing, just having a lot of clean fun. I didn't get home until probably four in the morning. I didn't talk to my mother after I got home, but later when I went to church people were waving me over. "How could you do that to your mother?" they all asked.

"What are you talking about?" I said.

"Your mother said that you didn't come in till four o'clock in the morning," they explained. "She said it on the radio this morning."

It was very embarrassing. I wondered how many other churches were aware of what I did. My mother has been a radio personality in Philadelphia for thirty-seven years. She hosts an all-gospel program and has developed a reputation and quite a name for herself. It was a double whammy for my brothers, my sister, and me: not only was our mother a public figure, but she was also a minister. She became ordained and started preaching in the late seventies. So you have the aspect of being the kids of a prominent figure in the community, but you are also a "preacher's kid" – all eyes are on you.

I guess there is an expectation that because you're the preacher's kid, you do not keep those kinds of hours on a day before you go to church. I realized then that I had to try to be a little smarter, and also that I had to talk to my mom to make sure she didn't do that again. "Ma," I said, "you can't say certain things on the air like that. Remember, we have lives we have to live too."

"Oh, did I say that," she said. "I didn't even realize it. I'm sorry." She tried to play the dummy role. Probably she just liked to talk. The program she hosts on Sundays is from six in the morning to two in the afternoon, and that's a lot of time to spend in front of the microphone.

I'm sure she had to find all kinds of little tidbits to share with the listening audience.

My mother never beat us over the head with "You can't do something because people are looking." She would squeeze it in there every now and then when appropriate. So it wasn't necessarily that I felt like I had to walk a superthin line, but I knew that news traveled back to my mother in ways I couldn't figure out. I remember visiting one of the black colleges for a homecoming, and me and my friends ended up just having a good time. That Monday morning when I got back my mother said, "I heard you were out there dancing. Somebody told me that they didn't think a preacher's son could dance like that." I said, "Mom, how are you getting these reports?" She just said, "You'd be surprised sometimes what I find out."

I also feel my siblings and I had a greater advantage in life because of my mother. Every time my mother was on the radio doing her gospel program, she'd spend a few moments in prayer. She would always ask the audience to join her in praying for her children, and she'd call each one of us by name. Even now I meet people and they'll say, "I used to pray for you back when your mother would mention your name on the radio." Her show was the number-one radio program on Sunday, so there were a lot of people listening and joining her in prayer. You figure that's a lot of prayers going up to the Master, so I'd better carry myself understanding that obligation.

Sometimes the visibility was a double-edged sword. I think when my mother and father divorced it was especially tough on my mother. Both of my parents were working at WDAS Radio. My father was also a radio personality. Like anyone else, you have aspects of your life that you want to keep private even if you are a public figure. But during the divorce there was a lot of talk.

It certainly wasn't *National Enquirer* news, but still, people talked about reasons for the divorce. That was hard. But one thing I say is my mother grew up on a dusty farm deep down in Georgia, a place called Cairo, near the border of Florida. She was accustomed to working hard and being focused on the goal. Early on I think she knew that the burden of raising us was going to be hers alone to bear. And she stepped up to the plate. That's not to say my father had no role at all; but he had other obligations and his involvement wasn't that day-in, day-out interaction that we had with our mother. I will never forget what she's done, because it wasn't easy.

We certainly didn't want for anything. She always tried to give us the extras. I remember we were going to buy a gift my brother wanted for his birthday. We went there to pick it out, and I guess it was expensive. Being young and wanting to have everything that my siblings had, I begged her for one too. I can

remember just the expression on her face, really contemplative, a "let me see if I can make this work" kind of look. She said, "Tell you what, I really don't have the money for this, but I'll get it for you." It was a simple gesture, but I think that was when I started being more sensitive to my mother's situation. Don't get me wrong, I took that gift. But after that, I really started being more careful about the things I asked for.

My mother would apologize to us when they'd have parent-teacher kinds of things and she couldn't go, because she worked so hard and was worn out. But she made sure we all got a solid education. She wore herself out trying to come up with money to make things happen. I was sickly as a child. I am a diabetic, and there were a few other things that kept me ill for a while. During the fifth and sixth grades I was in the hospital quite a bit, and my mother would be there every day, rain or shine. She spent that time talking with me and just giving love that only a mother can give. It really provided a sense of security.

My mother is a very supportive person in all areas. I think for her the biggest failure would be not trying. She believes you just never know till you try, and if you fail, then you just pick yourself up, dust yourself off, and try something else. My mother wasn't celebrating our failures, but she certainly wouldn't criticize us for them. Even if it was something that we brought on ourselves, that she warned us about, in her mind's eye it is more important to build people up than tear them down.

No matter what you do in life, you have to find your own place. I think everybody has their own special place and destiny, and you shouldn't be focused on standing in somebody else's shadow. I never deny who my mother is, I'm too proud of her, but in the same breath, I'd like to be appreciated for who I am. You've got to make a way for yourself and you've got to make a name for yourself. Don't get me wrong, I am proud of my mother because she has led a life that people respected. When people would see us, they'd ask, "Are you Louise's son? Oh, your mother is such a wonderful person." That still gives me a real sense of pride and appreciation. Should I ever have kids, I would certainly want them to hold their heads up and feel proud about me in the same way.

RON DAISE & KATHLEEN DAISE

VOICE FROM ON HIGH

Ron Daise's mother raised him with the values, morals, and beliefs of a unique American community. Daise grew up on St. Helena Island — one of the Sea Islands, located off the coast of South Carolina — a place where the culture brought with them by enslaved Africans centuries ago thrived and was transformed into a unique culture called Gullah. Kathleen Daise instilled in her son the teachings that had been passed down from generations before her: the importance of working hard, of providing a good home for one's family, and, above all, of keeping one's faith in God. ■ Daise has become one of the community's historians through his books and performance pieces about the Gullah culture. With his wife, Natalie, he stars in *Gullah Gullah Island*, a popular children's preschool program on Nickelodeon. The show's wholesome values reflect those of Daise's island upbringing, and have made him a father figure to thousands of children across the country. ■ Kathleen Daise expected her nine children to live up to their potential and meet the expectations of both family and community. At age eighty-four, she continues to remind her children — no matter how old they grow — not to stray too far from the fundamental belief system that has sustained them until now. Listening to Daise talk about his mother reinforced for me the idea that what we learn at home can carry us through life, a source of inspiration in practically anything — no matter how big or small — that we do.

RON DAISE
Writer/Performance Artist
AGE FORTY-ONE
MOTHER KATHLEEN DAISE

My parents' childbearing spanned twenty years. I was born when my mother was forty-two, the last of nine. I always felt that because I was born to my mother in her older age, one of my purposes was to help her. And in helping her do things around the house, I'd take notice of how she lived and the kinds of things that she did. One of the most important things that my mother instilled in me was the importance of prayer. And faith. Trusting in God to determine what's the best thing to do, and once you've made a decision with that in mind, you just step forward and go through it. "Though the going might get rough," my mother would say, "if God is with you it's all going to work out in the end."

I think my mother transmitted this sense of faith by demonstrating it herself. By living life. My mother told me, well, first of all when you have something to do, when you're working on something, you just pray about it. This is something that you need to do, and then you wait. When you get some impulse, an inclination to do something afterwards, you act on that because that's probably God's response for you. And when you do that, do the very best at it that you can. And afterwards, you say a prayer of thanks. That's how you do it.

Upon completing college, my first job was back home at the local newspaper, the Beaufort *Gazette*. Two years and three months into that job, I knew that wasn't what I wanted to do. But to some people it's a plum job. Here I was, the first black reporter ever at the *Gazette*, writing human interest stories about the elderly residents in the community. Some of the local islanders even called me the editor of the *Gazette*. I was making a nominal amount of money. But I knew there was something else, and because I knew that so strongly, I left. That really angered and frustrated a lot of people who thought I was walking away from something I was supposed to do for the rest of my life. But with the sense of self that my mother helped to instill in me, I knew that wasn't it. I knew it was time to move on to something else, not just be consumed in making something happen that wasn't really supposed to be. So I prayed about it, and it was done.

I think I have applied this to just about everything I do, even simple things. I used to trim the hedges at home, one of the chores to be done around the house. And my mother would say, when you trim the hedges, you stand back and you look at it. And then you see whatever design you want. And then you move in again. You watch the design. And then you'll have completed the job. Then people will pass by and they'll see those hedges. And they'll want to know who's done such a good job. And they'll ask you to do the same for them. So do a good job at whatever you do. I use this concept. If ever I have a project, an assignment, I look at what I'm doing as closely as possible and I do the very best I can.

My mother is a very wise woman, a very determined woman. I think knowing and accepting her place in life made her wise. And with that acceptance, knowing that there was a job to be done and doing it. And just loving life. My mother taught school before she began having children. When the children came, she thought the best thing was for her to stay home, even though I think there were other things she wanted to do, such as pursue higher education. So I always had a breakfast in the morning, I always had dinner, and my mom would attend any activities at school. If I was running track, my mother was there. If there was a PTO meeting, my mother was there. And she was that way with all nine of her children. That's why some people thought our family was rich. But we weren't — not hardly. But she made sure that she was present and active in our lives.

My father was a carpenter. He had a civil service job. We had a moderate income...well, moderate might be too high. We never had a car. My mother would catch rides or walk to those places to be present for us. She sacrificed. She made new clothes out of old ones. She taught us how to take care of our home. And she didn't have many material possessions. We had a home where there was love and where we were cared for. That was what she could give and what she gave.

My father died when I was nine. He just slept away. He was fifty-two. I remember my mother and two older sisters had gone to a graduation service at St. Helena High School. It was on May 30. My older brother Stanley and I had been playing around the yard and in the house with other friends from the neighborhood. It was a Sunday afternoon and Dad was trying to sleep. He told us to be quiet. I guess that we had gotten too rambunctious. That was his announcement to us: "Please keep quiet, I am trying

to sleep." We were outside playing when Mom returned home, then there was this outcry, "Henry! Henry is gone! Henry done gone!" She was crying. Then the two sisters who were with her came in and told us, "Daddy's dead." All the children scattered. After that, people started coming in. Being a rural community, that's what people do when someone dies, they all start gathering around.

After his death, my mother had to become the provider. Mom became Dad as well as mother to us. It was a matter of enduring. There were children to raise. There was an annuity because of Dad's job, but it wasn't very much, something like $2,000 a year. Filling out financial assistance forms for college was always quite easy…it was like, zero, zero, zero, zero, zero. We owned a house and the land around it, and that was it. My mother began doing some part-time work, but for the most part she remained at home. We made do with what we had. It was hard, but Mama still managed to go to our events, giving the same kind of support she gave before Dad died. She always stressed to us that we were a family. We would all work in the summer, and we were all to look out for one another.

My mother had high expectations. She wanted us to treat each other and others fairly, for us to be honest. She wanted us to always do our best, and to be purposeful. She expected us to apply ourselves. She expected us to be at church on Sunday mornings. My mother had a vision of what's best for her children, and she moved forward with it no matter the circumstances, and she was unconditional in her love for us.

My mother recognized that I had talents and gifts. She's the one who told me my smile was beautiful. That was one of those growing up issues. I always considered myself very friendly, but people would say, "You smile too much." Or I wasn't as rough and tough as I needed to be. So I just stopped smiling. I was supposed to be more manly, I guess. But my mother told me, "You have a very beautiful smile. I like when you smile, and you should smile." And so I did. It was my mother telling me how much she loved it, how beautiful it was, that made me smile again. She was the one who instilled a joy of life in me. She wanted me to use whatever I had in a God-honoring manner.

Whatever level of success I might attain, my mother will always be quick to say, "You stay on your knees and be thankful for whatever accomplishments you have made. You stay on your knees, because it may not always be that way tomorrow or some-where down the line. There will be a change. Whether good or bad, there will be a new situation to deal with. But just remember that God is there. And with God you can deal with anything." I keep that with me always.

CHAZ GUEST & ALGIRTHA GUEST

A vast majority of the men I spoke to named faith in God as their mother's main source of strength and the reason she was able to endure hardship. Chaz Guest has always been awed by his mother's faith, and he knows that the church and its members have been a vital support system for her. The church was there for her when she had no one else to turn to. ■ Guest took his own leap of faith to pursue what he considers his God-given talent. He is a self-trained artist, who completed his first painting in 1990 at the age of twenty-eight. Since then, his work has been exhibited in galleries in New York and Los Angeles, and several pop and jazz artists have commissioned him to paint their portraits. Despite these accomplishments, though, he considers his greatest masterpiece his three-year-old son, Zuhri. After spending nearly a year tracking down Zuhri's mother, who had disappeared with the boy, Guest truly cherishes having him as a part of his family. He recently moved to California to be closer to Zuhri, but he makes an effort to bring the boy back east to be with his grandmother as often as possible. He wants his son to know her as intimately as he does. ■ Algirtha Guest's faith in God has made her fearless, always prepared to do the right thing no matter how dangerous it may seem, and her example has made Chaz Guest equally fearless. Their story demonstrates the power and impact of a mother's faith on her family, and the essential support it provides when they need it most.

CHAZ GUEST
Artist
AGE THIRTY-SIX
MOTHER ALGIRTHA GUEST

My mother's on the God squad. She really loves God, man. It's unbelievable. In my family it was always church, church, church. You woke up in the morning and you got ready for church. Three days a week and all day on Sunday. The only requirement we had to adhere to was to be there and stay awake. But that was a job. First of all, I didn't want to go. Secondly, once I got there I wanted to sleep, which was out of the question. I may be a backslider or whatever you call it, but I believe in God because of my mother. She believes that God is on her side. And you know what? he must be. I know he must be, because we lived on the edge and all of her nine children are still alive. I really believe that God has watched over her and does so still. Whatever she believes in, I will too, because I have seen it work for her.

My father was a very well known minister in Niagara Falls. We had this big house and a boat there. We lived very close to the falls, and we could walk to Canada. My life was about grass, worms for fishing, and water; it was full of nature and a lot of church. We did everything together. Our family was like the Partridge Family. It really was, until I was about ten, when my parents separated. They had been together for maybe sixteen years. Whatever they had going on, they had to break up. Now

that I'm a man, and a single father, I don't pry. I understand that when a man and a woman don't get along, someone has to split.

My mother took her nine children to live in Philadelphia on her own. She orchestrated the move very well. Half of us went over to Mrs. Bell's house, the others went over to Mrs. Johnson's. The next thing I knew we were standing in front of a Greyhound bus holding a bucket of chicken, on our way to Philadelphia. My father had gone shopping, and when he came back we were gone. I remember looking out of the bus window. I was eating a chicken leg and thinking, where am I going? My mother had worked out every-thing from Niagara Falls. When we got to Philadelphia, the church there took us in threes. Three sisters went to Sister Brown's house; the boys went to Brother Brown's house; and my mother and the rest of the kids stayed with someone else until she found a house.

The church became her safe haven and she was dedicated to it. She was in the choir and it was like a family. There was a sisterhood in the church that was pretty thick, and those women became like aunts to me. If it wasn't for the church, I don't think my mother would have been as successful. I have one child, and I can't imagine how she cared for and raised nine children alone.

My mother maintained the same discipline in Philadelphia as she did before we moved. You dare not miss church, and I don't think I ever missed. I was never defiant, I never said I'm not going. I never did that. When I heard somebody swear at their mother, I could not believe it. I almost fell out. That's the level of respect that we had for our mother, and that's the level of respect that she demanded, in a very loving way. It wasn't heavy-handed. She did hit me once, because I got my hair braided. That was the only time I remember.

My mother worked as a nurse's aide up to the time she retired. All she did was work and take care of her children. I used to hate to see her in that white uniform going to work, because it was dangerous. She always had to work the night shift and catch the subway late at night to the hospital in the city. I was very concerned about her. But my mother taught me not to worry. She always said to me that she's just passing through. But now that she's retired, it's my job to do something for her. It's my job is to try to become very successful so I can take care of her the way she took care of us growing up.

Everything my mother did, she never asked for anything in return. I remember one Christmas she laid out seven dollars apiece on the bed for us, seven dollars times nine. She called each of us up to her room, and we went up and took the money. I didn't want it. I remember giving her back five dollars and I kept two. I had never seen my mother buy herself anything. She worked every night just to make sure you had before she had for herself. I always thought she could have been a damn good doctor, because she is very smart and loves to help people. I always thought if she had been an educated woman, she would really be something else.

My mother protected us by keeping us in church. But she would do anything for her children. She'd kick someone's ass for her children if she had to. She'd take off her high-heeled shoes and that church hat, and braid her hair and throw down, and then go to church the next day. I witnessed it with my own eyes. At the time, gang wars were really heavy. My brother is a martial artist, so for him to have been recruited into a gang would have been like getting Bill Gates

to join your computer firm. One day my brother was in trouble. The gang members were trying to beat him up, but he was kicking everybody's ass. This one guy picked up a two-by-four and was getting ready to swing it at my brother's head. My mother was walking down the street and saw what was going on. She ran and jumped on the guy's back. Then she grabbed her son and yelled to all of them, "Y'all need to go to church!" My mother could fight. She used to wrestle goats on the farm where she grew up. She's built like a linebacker — not fat, just muscles. Strong.

When my mother bought the duplex where she lives now, the neighborhood was going down. The projects opened up across the street and there were gangs, drug traffic, and garbage on the street. My mother would go out there and say, "You-all are animals. Why do you throw trash on the street? I'm going to call the people to give you a fine." And she'd call, and they would get fined. If somebody drove by with their boom box, she would say, "Turn that music down! People live on this block!" I guess she'd treat everybody like they were her children — and if you don't behave, I'm going to call the cops. She didn't care if people liked her; she didn't care if they threatened her. We always told her, if you're gonna call the cops on the drug dealers, don't give them your name. She'd say okay. Then she'd dial 9-1-1 and go right ahead and say, "Hello, this is Algirtha Guest and I want to report some drug dealers."

She got people in City Hall to pay attention to the area. Now they patrol the place and all the cops know Algirtha. She's a trip. She always says, "Chaz, it takes one person to make a difference." My mother has these sayings, like "There has to be one big rat to make the hole for the little rats to get through." They are really funny. My mother has a way of making everything sound easy, but the truth is she was persistent and she cleaned up the block single-handedly.

Nobody really did anything to threaten my mother physically. It's just that she has this thing about helping people that could be dangerous sometimes. A lot of people are on crack now, and sometimes there's trouble. My mother rents the upstairs apartment of her duplex. I remember this one lady who was doing crack. My mother called the police on her and they took her away. Then she took the lady's son into the apartment. It bothers me when she puts her life in jeopardy like that, but I have to believe that she's taken care of. She truly believes God is on her side. If there is anyone who is proof of the power of God, it's my mother. I love her for that. She's like a saint. When I hear stories about other people's mothers and their situations, I thank God for Algirtha. I have a real mother, and the older I get, the more in awe of her I become. They don't make women like that anymore. My mother is like a piece of God's light.

B E N J A M I N   C A R S O N   &   S O N Y A   C A R S O N

Although Dr. Benjamin Carson credits God and his mother for his success in life, he says education played a key role. In fact, the majority of men in this collection cited their mother's emphasis on education as having the greatest impact on their lives. They recalled their mothers helping them with their homework, attending parent-teacher meetings, defending them if they were given an unfair grade – all significant gestures that helped their sons achieve. Of all the stories, however, Dr. Benjamin Carson's most dramatically illustrates the lengths to which a mother will go to make sure her sons receive the full benefit of education. ■ Sonya Carson has watched her elder son, Curtis, go on to become a successful engineer with Allied Signal, and Benjamin, one of the most celebrated neurosurgeons in the world. Dr. Carson is the director of pediatric neuro-surgery at Johns Hopkins Medical Center, and has received national and international acclaim for his part in the first successful separation of Siamese twins joined at the head – an operation that took five months to plan and required twenty-two hours of surgery. Dr. Carson lives outside Baltimore, Maryland, with his wife and three sons. His mother lives with them, in a private wing of their home. ■ Carson's mother was dedicated to her children's success, but that dedication came with consequences. Dr. Carson believes she gave up her youth and much more for her children. Carson makes it his business to talk to children in schools and youth centers around the country about his life and what it takes to overcome hardship, and he never forgets to thank her.

BENJAMIN CARSON
Pediatric Neurosurgeon
AGE FORTY-THREE
MOTHER SONYA CARSON

My parents divorced when I was eight years old, and there were a lot of rumors. My father was telling people that the divorce was my mother's fault. But my mother never told anyone what was really going on, that my father had another family. She was not a person who spent a lot of time talking to people. She didn't go out and defend herself. She just said, "It's really nobody else's business." But learning of my father's bigamy and the split up were very difficult for my mother. I think trying to hold all of that in, and looking at how bleak the future looked after she had worked so hard to try to make something of her and my father's life, was too much. She became very depressed and had to be admitted to a psychiatric hospital on more than one occasion. We never knew that as youngsters, because she would simply tell us that she had to go away on business. She'd arrange for friends, neighbors, or relatives to take care of us for a week or two. But actually she was being checked into a facility for treatment of severe depression. She was very good at keeping that stuff from us. It was only many years later that she told us what was going on.

Occasionally we would see our father. He was supposed to be paying alimony, but getting that out of him was very difficult. My mother went to court many, many times, and he would pay for a little while and then he would stop. I didn't hold any grudges or harsh feeling toward my father, I think partly because my mother seldom blamed him, at least not to us. After a while she just said the heck with it, "I'll do whatever I have to do." We were very poor after he left us. The three of us, my mother, my brother, and I, would go out in the country on Sunday mornings, and she would knock on farmers' doors. "Can me and my boys pick four bushels of beans or greens?" she would ask. "Three will be for you, and we'll take one as payment." Then she would take our bushel home and can it. We would go out to wild fields and pick grapes and apples, and she'd come home and can those, make jellies and preserves and stuff to last through the winter. My mother was one of those people who really knew how to scrimp and save and get the most out of every possible thing. She would go to the Goodwill and buy a twenty-five-cent shirt and get a pack of buttons and some patches and fix it up. She would save any extra money she made as a domestic, under the mattress or wherever, and drive a car until it basically wouldn't run anymore. Then she'd take the money out from under her mattress and buy a new car. And people would say, "Wait a minute, how can that women have a new car? She must be doing something on the side." There were always these rumors circulating about my mother. But she was just extraordinarily thrifty.

With all of that, my mother still never said, "Poor me," which was good. But the bad thing was, she never felt sorry for me or my brother, either. She always held our feet to the fire. There was never such a thing as a good excuse.

She always quoted this poem, "Yourself to Blame":

> *...You're the captain of your ship.*
> *When things go awry, don't blame others.*
> *You have yourself to blame....*

And whenever an excuse came out of your mouth, you could be sure that poem was on its way. So after a while you just stopped looking for excuses and started looking for ways to get things done. The most important thing my mother passed on to me and my brother is that she never considered herself a victim.

My mother is a very attractive woman. There was no end of suitors, men were always pursuing her. But she made it clear to them that as far as she was concerned, her main job in life was to make sure that her sons got a head start in life. She worked two and three jobs at a time. She would leave very early in the morning and get back very late at night, so we learned how to take care of ourselves. We were latch-key kids. She would have food prepared, and we learned how to warm it up. At a fairly early age, we learned how to be pretty independent. But my mother still tried to find time to spend with us. She would make sure that we had places to go, particularly free places. She played baseball with us, she was out there playing volleyball, going on hikes — whatever we were playing, she was playing. She tried to be there for us.

My brother and I both had severe problems at school. We were doing incredibly poorly. In fact, I was by far the worst in my class. The kids used to call me dummy. That was my nickname. The kids thought I was dumb, the teachers thought I was dumb, I thought I was dumb. My mother was the only person who didn't. "You're smart," she was always saying. "You're very smart, much too smart to be bringing home grades like this." She encouraged

us, but she really didn't know how to get us going. She felt that we were going to end up like her, just working hard for somebody else all our lives and never having anything, and never being in control of our own lives. So she just prayed and asked God to somehow show her what she could do to get us on the right track. And that's when she came up with the idea of turning off the TV and making us read two books apiece from the library and submit written book reports to her. We started submitting the book reports to her, but we didn't know she couldn't read. She only had a third-grade education at the time. She never let us know, and we kept on submitting the book reports. After about three weeks I began to enjoy it. It got to the point where I couldn't wait to get home and get into my books. I was reading like a fiend, and my brother was too. Pretty soon my mother didn't have to do anything. We didn't want to watch TV, we wanted to read our books every chance we got. People started to think we were really weird.

Very rapidly I began to enjoy the acquisition of knowledge. All of a sudden a teacher would ask a question and I would be the only one who knew the answer. Wow, this is heavy, I said to myself. I suddenly had an insatiable thirst for knowledge. My mother's friends were telling her that her sons would hate her, that they would grow up to be sissies, that they wouldn't be able to do anything. "You can't keep boys in the house reading," they would say to her. But she wasn't about to listen. She wanted much more for her sons. She truly believed at that point that education was the key to escape poverty, to escape from desperation.

Within the space of a year and a half, I went from the bottom of the class to the top, much to the consternation of all the students who were calling me dummy. They now were the ones who were coming to me and saying, how do you do this, how do you do that, how do you work this problem? I would say, sit at my feet, youngster, while I instruct you. I was pretty obnoxious, but it was fun. I became the know-it-all. If I took a test and got an A, but somebody else got an A that was higher than my A, I was devastated. I couldn't wait until the next test when I could get a higher A than they did.

When I was eight years old, listening to mission stories in school, I realized that I wanted to be a doctor. Missionary doctors seemed like the noblest people in the world, going out at great personal sacrifice to bring physical, mental, and spiritual health to people. I said, "That's what I want to do."

"Benny, you can do anything you want," my mother told me. "You're a smart boy, and all you have to do is apply yourself and trust in the Lord. And you can be any kind of doctor you want to be. Not only will you be a doctor, but you'll

229

be the best. You'll be the best there ever was."

I heard that over and over, year after year, report card after report card. And after a while, I did start to believe that maybe I really was smart. It was a combination of the reading and knowing answers that other people didn't know, and then hearing my mother say, "You're much smarter than everybody," that did it. I couldn't help but believe it. I mean, she brainwashed us.

My mother worked in the homes of wealthy people as a domestic. And she was very observant. She saw how they lived and what they did. She would come home and say, these people own this and they own that, and they don't watch TV all the time. They're always reading. And the way they conduct themselves — they're very kindly. They believe in getting things done. She would actually take us out to the neighborhoods where they lived. We saw beautiful, manicured lawns and homes, and then we'd come back to where we lived and see people bumming around on the street, and she would say, "Now you have a choice. Cast your lot here or cast your lot there. The choice is yours."

I never resented my mother being a maid and taking care of other people's households, because she didn't resent it. She looked at it as an opportunity. She saw it as a stepping-stone. So many people today who find themselves in a desperate situation would say, "I'm not doing that. That's beneath me. I can't do that." And they never go anywhere, because they can't climb up the ladder. They want to start at the top of the ladder, but it doesn't work that way. You have to take the opportunities as they come and do a good job with what you're given, and then you're given more. Nothing was too lowly for my mother. That was something she understood, and she passed it on to us.

My mother is a very, very important factor in developing the philosophies I have: the work ethic, the non-victim's mentality, the can-do spirit. She never admitted that there was something that couldn't be done. "Mr. 'I Can't' died," she always said. Whatever it is, you can do it. You just got to find a way. And that has tremendously influenced my career. My mother was willing to sacrifice her life for us. And she did. From the time she was in her twenties, she didn't live for herself. I'd say she lost her life. That's a lot. It brings tears to my eyes when I think about it.

My mother didn't have to have the hard life she had. She could have married one of those suitors, and some of them were doing very well. She would have been well taken care of. But they didn't particularly care about her young sons and that's exactly why she didn't do it. She would rather live in poverty and work three jobs to make sure that her sons got what they needed. That's what she chose to do.

ERIC H. HOLDER JR. & MIRIAM HOLDER

A̲ll the men I interviewed said their mothers had high expectations for them. Some mothers asked only that their sons be responsible, good people; others were more specific, and encouraged their sons to choose a particular profession. Whether or not those expectations were met, they remained a motivating factor in the men's lives. In Eric H. Holder Jr.'s case, his mother was the driving force behind his success in becoming the highest-ranking black in law enforcement in the history of the country. Miriam Holder herself graduated only from high school, and Holder always knew she had higher aspirations for him. ■ Both Holder's mother and his father, the late Eric H. Holder Sr., have roots in the Caribbean island of Barbados. Holder describes his childhood as a combination of traditional West Indian values and an American Ozzie and Harriet upbringing of the 1950s. He now has a family of his own, which looks a little like the TV Cosby family of the 1980s: his wife is a doctor of obstetrics and gynecology, and the couple has three children, two daughters and a son. ■ Through college, law school, and subsequent careers as a practicing lawyer and a judge, Holder has relied repeatedly on his mother's practical advice and common sense. Now as deputy attorney general of the United States, Holder continues to seek her counsel. In her, Holder has had a lifelong mentor – one full of unconditional love and support. This mother-son relationship shows what a strong motivator and counselor a mother can be to her son, no matter how great his success becomes.

ERIC H. HOLDER JR.
United States Deputy Attorney General
AGE FORTY-SIX
MOTHER MIRIAM HOLDER

My mother never really came out and said it, but there was this unspoken urging: "I expect big things from you, Eric Holder Junior" I think the reason was because I was capable. My mother always encouraged me. If I was down about something, if I got a bad grade in school, if I didn't do well in an athletic event, she always found a way to put a good spin on it. When you were young, she made it so perhaps you didn't cry as long as you might have, and if you were an adolescent and something went wrong, you didn't feel as badly as you might have. I always had the belief that I didn't want to disappoint her, that it was my responsibility to work hard, to take advantage of opportunities that I was given and not let obstacles stand in my way.

I never had the feeling that my mother would let me accept the easy way out, that a B would be okay when I was capable, if I worked hard, of getting an A. I never had the sense from my mother that it would have been acceptable if I had decided to leave my career as a judge and go live on a beach in Barbados. She would never say, "I don't want you to do that," but she would make it quite clear in her own way that this was inconsistent with her vision of what her boy should be doing in the world. She always gave my brother and me freedom to decide what we wanted to do, and yet she has a certain facial expression that she gets. "Well, if that's what you'd like to do," she says as she puts her hand on her chin, "I mean, I can understand that." Then she goes from there. "Are you sure that's what you want to do? I can understand that. Now why do you say you want to do that?" She'd get you to talk it out, directing the conversation in such a way that ultimately you decide yourself that this isn't something that you want to do. She would have been a good lawyer!

To the extent that she could, my mother did not allow me to deviate from the path she thought I should be on. I went to a specialized high school, Stuyvesant, in New York. It was a very intellectually rigorous place. I took the entrance test, got in, and went. In the first couple of weeks I just didn't like it. I had to travel from Queens to Manhattan, probably an hour and a half every day. There weren't a lot of black kids there, and I didn't like the teachers. So I decided quickly that I wanted to transfer to our local high school, which my mother saw as turning my back on a really good educational opportunity. Over the course of a month or so, on almost a daily basis, she did two things: She was the nice mom, putting her arm around me and saying, "You can do this, it'll be okay." At the same time, she had her hand on my back, pushing me towards what she thought was the right thing. I've never been good with transitions, even as an adult. If not for her intervention, I would have missed what was probably the single most important educational experience I had. A lot of the success that I've had is based on the three years that I spent at Stuyvesant. Her sensitivity and insistence got me through.

My mother is a friend and confidante. She's a person who only went to high school, but I will ask her for her advice. I can't always tell her specifically what I'm talking about because some of it's secret, but I've asked her advice on some important things. "What do you think I should do in this case, Mom?" I've done that all my life. She's a good barometer. If I have ideas about projects, and I want to get a sense of how people are going to react generally and how black folks are going to react in particular, I'll pitch the idea or concept to her. She's got a good feel of how people are going to react to stuff.

She has always had the ability to make you feel special. As a kid it was a very good thing to have a mother who was not stingy with her praise and who was always giving, who was never at a loss for time. She always found a way to give us attention. She was also sensitive to what it was like to be a young guy

growing up, and at the time I think I took it for granted. Now I see a lot of this as being relatively extraordinary.

My mother had the ability to deal with us as young guys. She knew what it meant to be an adolescent, to be thirteen, fourteen, fifteen years old and gawky and not sure of yourself. She made me and my brother feel confident in a way that you might not expect of a woman. I think she sensitized us. I guess you'd have to talk to my wife and women I've gone out with to confirm it, but I learned a lot from my mother, who was always concerned about how I was interacting with the people I was going out with, and that I was being nice to them. She was concerned if I was breaking up with them, how was it happening. I think I'm a pretty sensitive guy, and if I am, it's due in no small part to her.

Both my mother and father come from very strong black women. Among the two strongest women I've ever known are my grandmothers, tough women,

both of whom had it rough. My grandfather on my mother's side died of tuberculosis when my mother was about four or five years old, leaving her mother with two kids. My grandmother had to go to work. My mother had to go live with relatives for a while, until her mother got set up and was able to come back to Atlantic City. My father's mother left him in Barbados, came to New York and established herself, and then brought him, and later his sister, over with her. The women on my mother's side of the family are all really strong-willed traditional women. When I say traditional, I mean centered around the home. And they are not shy at all about sharing their opinions; my mother's sisters, aunts, cousins, are all like that, and I think that is the foundation for any success that I've had. It's a tough thing to be a black guy in this country. It has been, it is, and in the foreseeable future it will continue to be. Without people in your corner, and chief among them your parents, and chief among your parents, your mom, life is difficult.

The sense my mother imbued in me was that I was capable, that I could compete. She told me that things were not necessarily going to be easy for me because I was black, but that was just something I had to deal with, and whether fair or unfair, it could not be used as an excuse. She did this always with a sense that you were capable, and no matter what the obstacle, you could somehow overcome it. You just had to figure it out.

I can remember in the late fifties, early sixties, sitting with my mother watching the civil rights struggles in the South and the march on Washington on television. I remember her talking about what was happening and pointing things out to me. I can't remember my conversations with her, but I remember she had really strong negative reactions to the news stories about what was going on in the South.

I came out of my time with my parents strengthened, able to handle the racial stuff I've had to handle. Some people get crippled by racism and are unable to function. Some people get crippled by it and become hypersensitive. I think my mother got me onto a stable middle ground, proud and very conscious of who I am, realistic in my view of the world and how the world perceives me. I might be the U.S. deputy attorney general, but the reality is I'm a black U.S. deputy attorney general. And I understand the added pressure and expectations that come with it from all sides.

All the love, all the nurturing, all the confidence-building that my mother gave me, are the right of every child. All too frequently, it's not given to black kids, and in particular, young black guys. In a perfect world you have a father and mother who care about you. In the imperfect world, we see fathers who are too often absent and mothers who are raising kids without the tools my mother had. I think it's a question of having the time and the desire to give the attention that children need. I'm a father now, and I really appreciate how difficult it can be when you're tired and your kids are asking you the same questions for the fifth or sixth time. But I never got from my mother a sense that I was a pain, that I was a burden. She put in the time and made me and my brother always feel special.

My mother is a very bright woman. I believe that in a different time, my mother's career would have been like mine. She would have gone to an Ivy League school and been a lawyer, a doctor, or whatever. I don't think my mother regrets the way life unfolded for her, because I think that she looks at me and my brother, who is a police lieutenant for the Port Authority, and sees in us the fruition of some of the dreams she had for herself. That's why she gets particular joy out of me being the new U.S. deputy attorney general. When I got sworn in as a judge, I was not married at the time, and my mother held the Bible for me. She cried through that ceremony. She always says I make her proud, and that is very important to me. Even now, at forty-six years old, I get a great deal of pleasure knowing that I've done something that makes my mom feel good.

239

NOEL MACNEAL & EDNA MACNEAL

Noel MacNeal is no stranger to expectations. It's just that his mother's were a bit more general

than most. Edna MacNeal wanted her son to enjoy his childhood while he could and to then pursue

whatever career would make him happy in life. Although she sacrificed her own ambitions to give her

son this kind of freedom, she did it without burdening him with guilt and without the expectation of

anything in return. Under her selfless guidance, MacNeal took what he loved to do as a child and

turned it into a successful career as a puppeteer. ▪ You may not know MacNeal by sight — he's usually

fully costumed when he works — but children definitely know the characters he has brought to life on

television: Mrs. Snuffleupagus on *Sesame Street*, Magellan the Dragon on Nickelodeon's *Eureka's Castle*,

Leon on *The Puzzle Place*, and, most recently, the Bear in the Disney Channel's *Bear in the Big Blue*

House. Sometimes his mother visits the studio and watches him in action. She even got a chance to

revisit her acting interests by making cameo appearances on some of his shows. ▪ MacNeal says

almost apologetically that there is no pain and suffering in his story. He and his mother enjoy each

other's company and respect each other's lives. Neither one of them presses the other to do any-

thing but have fun. Edna MacNeal raised a dreamer on purpose, enabling her son to stretch his

imagination and find his life's work — which just happens to make children all over the world happy.

NOEL MACNEAL
Puppeteer
AGE THIRTY-SIX
MOTHER EDNA MACNEAL

My grandmother and my mother were two very proud black women. They instilled confidence in me. I was taught to first make sure you're right, then go ahead. That was almost the family motto: go ahead, and whatever you do, be proud of it. I knew I wanted to be a puppeteer since I was a little kid. I always played with puppets, made puppets. It was not until *The Muppet Show* came on television when I was in high school and I realized that this guy Jim Henson and all of these people were making a living from puppets that I said, why can't I? The guidance counselor at high school gave me more of a hassle about becoming a puppeteer than my mother did. "Shouldn't you do something more concrete?" he said. "No, this is what I want to do," I said, "and this is the way I want to do it."

I remember when I told my mother I wanted to go to college to be a puppeteer, I was prepared. I had done my research, and I told her there were two colleges I could choose from because they had puppetry courses. She said, "Okay, what do we have to do?"

"Well, these are the applications right here." I showed them to her.

"When are they due back?" she asked, and I told her. That was the extent of the conversation. I never heard, "This is good, but what's your fallback course for a real job?" It was always, go for it! I would ask her from time to time, "You sure you want me to do this?" But I didn't have to convince her or steamroll her, or connive and campaign. There was no hesitation. This came from a woman who had dreams of her own but circumstance prevented her from going for it.

I grew up in Lennox Terrace, one of the finest apartment developments in Harlem. We had a six-room apartment with a doorman. We had a terrace that had a view of downtown Manhattan. So, compared to everyone else around us, we were living pretty well. My mom still lives up there. Dad wasn't around at all. He left when I was a baby, so basically my mom raised me with the help of my grandma. I knew we were different from the typical American family, because there wasn't mom and dad and kids and a dog living in a house. It was me, Mom, my grandmother, and my uncle living in an apartment. But that didn't mean that we weren't proud of who we were and what we accomplished.

Mom worked seven days a week in order to put me through private school. She worked as a corporate typist Monday through Friday. And on weekend afternoons she worked at an answering service. Mom put food on the table and we always had presents for Christmas. I always wanted to get an odd job, but she didn't want that. She wanted better for me. I would occasionally do a puppet show, only because that's what I wanted to do. She was adamant: "No, no, no. Concentrate on your puppetry and schoolwork. You don't have to do work."

Mom wanted to be an actress. She studied acting with this young actor named Sidney Poitier, who was setting up his own little studio. She and Sidney and a couple other students would get together once a week and go through scenes. He was their instructor. One of the other guys in this class was a kid who had torn sneakers and never enough money to buy his own dinner. She would often take him home and have her mother cook him a decent meal. The kid's name was Billy Dee Williams. My mother ended up putting the acting on hold and eventually just let it go. Reality kicked in; she got married and became pregnant. She also saw more starving actors than successful ones in the group that she was hanging out with, and we needed money.

One time, Sidney Poitier was walking down the street in New York City. My mother was walking toward him, and stayed right in his face. She said you could see that he was wondering, who is this woman and why is she staring at me? It finally clicked. "Oh, my God! Edna!" he yelled, and hugged her. Everybody in the street knew who he was, and they were trying to figure out, who in the hell is she, Oprah?

My mother is not shy at all and could charm the pants off you. I bring her around my friends and they all immediately like her. I told my mother a long time ago, "You don't act like a mother." I wonder sometimes if anybody has the kind of mother I have. The woman cannot cook to save her life. For years I thought I grew up with Cajun food, until I realized my mother was just burning everything. There was no such thing as blackened chicken, it was burnt. My grandmother taught me to cook. She said, "In case anything happens to me, I don't want my only grandchild to starve to death." These days Mom never asks what I want for dinner. She'll ask, "Where do you want to go for dinner?" I'll ask her, "What are you making, Mom?" She'll answer, "Reservations."

I never went camping. Mom's idea of roughing it was a hotel without twenty-four-hour concierge service. She just likes the good things in life, and if you've got the money and somebody else is willing to do the service for you, great. She loves buying clothes, dressing well. Loves Chanel No. 5. No cheap stuff for Mom.

We have a mutual respect and appreciation for each other. We're the only family we have right now. We're the only ones left and pretty much the only ones that really matter. That's why we're really close and have been for as long as I can remember. She's always been fun to hang out with and very easy to get along with. We do brunch once a week, on Sundays, just to catch up. I talk to my mother once a day just to say Hi. She'll stop by if she's in my neighborhood, and sometimes when I get home there will be a note saying, "Just dropped by, sorry we missed you." She respects who I am and what I've done, and I respect her and what she has had to do. She doesn't say, why aren't you doing this or why aren't you doing that. And I'm not pushing her away.

Last year on her sixty-fifth birthday I took Mom to Disney World and invited a couple of friends down. We had her celebration at Epcot. There's a hotel complex nearby where you can rent a pontoon boat and they'll take you out on Epcot's lake to watch the fireworks display. I called and explained it was my mom's birthday, and for no extra charge they had this beautiful birthday cake. We were out on the lake, singing "Happy Birthday" to my mom and watching the fireworks. People on the bridge applauded and wished her a happy birthday, and then as we're heading back the engine stalls. It just died, and we started drifting towards the weeds. Now, anybody else might have been screaming or bitching a blue streak about how

her birthday was ruined and we're not gonna pay a dime for this. My mom loved it. She was laughing the entire time. "Now this is a birthday I'm gonna remember," she said. The driver ended up ripping off the top of the table my mother's cake was on and using it as a paddle to get us across the lake. My mom was just sitting there with her legs crossed. "Oh yeah, this will make a good story," she said.

My mother believes in life, and living it now. What's the great phrase..."now is forever and tomorrow is just a lie"? That's her: you've got it right now, go for it now. She believes in education, she believes in hard work, and she believes that everyone should have a chance. She always emphasized that you can do whatever you want as long as it doesn't hurt anybody, and as long as you don't end up being a murderer, because, quote: I love you, darling, but I'd have to turn you in. She reminds me every now and then, "Life is too short to be miserable and to make other people miserable at the same time. Anytime you want to change careers, you can."

This from a woman who had to deal with working on a job that she hated for many years. She hated typing, because it was just a job. She worked seven days a week, not because she wanted to but because she had to, and that's why she would say, "You can always get a job. Get a career." And it was true. She had a job, but no one wants to make a career out of typing.

My mother may have hated typing, but because her initials had to go on the bottom of each letter she typed, she made sure it was the best letter that an executive got. She'd always say, if you're not proud enough to put your name on something, then something's wrong. "No matter what you do," she said, "if you dig ditches, be proud of it."

My mother deserves a good life. Now she wants to have an odd job the same way I wanted one as a kid. She thinks that she can help out and get a part-time job. And I'm like, "No, no, no. You concentrate on having fun. Relax. Go to the library." I want to make sure she doesn't want for anything, because it is her turn now. She's retired...well, she says she is "semiretired." It's a phrase she came up with. For her, retired means the end, you're ready to die. So she's semiretired. There was a time when she was thinking of relocating to Florida. But now she quotes a comedian, saying, "Florida is God's waiting room." She's not going anywhere anytime soon.

247

Sacred Bond

GEORGE C. WOLFE & ANNA MARY LINDSAY WOLFE

INTO ETERNITY

Growing up, George C. Wolfe received mixed messages from his mother, Anna Mary Lindsay Wolfe. She had traditional expectations of him – he was supposed to be a doctor or lawyer – yet she encouraged his creativity with complete abandon. Little did she know then that his passion for theater would lead to a place in Broadway history. ▪ Wolfe is the first African American to sit at the helm of the Joseph Papp Public Theater, one of the nation's most prestigious cultural institutions. He has written, directed, and produced some of the biggest commercial and critical hits on Broadway, among them *Bring in 'Da Noise, Bring in 'Da Funk, Angels in America,* and *Jelly's Last Jam.* Named a living landmark by the New York Landmarks Conservancy, Wolfe has garnered many honors, including numerous Tony, Drama Desk, Obie, and Audelco awards. ▪ Wolfe recognizes the influence of his mother, his father, his grandmother, and members of his childhood community in all that he has become in his life. But it was the special relationship with his mother that brought clarity, focus, and drive to his life. Until her death two years ago, she was always his most ardent supporter, a loyal protector, and above all, a proud mother. Their relationship is one Wolfe holds as dear now as he did while she was alive. In fact, he says she's never left him. Wolfe leaves us with an illuminating message: the bond between a black man and his mother endures beyond death and into eternity.

GEORGE C. WOLFE
Producer/Director/Writer
AGE FORTY-THREE
MOTHER ANNA MARY LINDSAY WOLFE

My mother passed away two years ago, three days before her birthday and about three weeks before my parents' fiftieth anniversary. She had been sick for a long time, about two years. She had a lot of heart trouble, then a series of strokes began taking away pieces of her. My mother loved to talk and she loved being around people. And she loved her mobility. So once the mobility and speech were gone, you knew she was miserable. She was not happy without those things that were so much of who and what she was.

Everything on the planet was going on in my life during that period. I was conceiving *Bring in 'Da Noise, Bring in 'Da Funk* and directing *Tempest* on Broadway at the exact same time. So on Mondays, my day off, I'd fly down to Texas to see my mother. It was just one of those extraordinary times. All of these unbelievable, incredible things were happening in my life while the most awful things were happening at the exact same time. I can't say how it affected me. I live so much in a state of denial that who in the hell can tell. At some point, when I'm sixty-nine, I'll go, what happened? But right now it's, just keep moving, keep moving – one of the things that I think I got from my mother. If a monsoon or a tornado strikes, you just keep walking. No matter what's going on, you just do what you're supposed to do. That's what my mother did. The last full sentence she ever said to me was so amazing, because it was when she was no longer able to make sentences. She said, "I know you want me to talk, baby, but I can't." That was her last sentence.

My mother and I had another kind of relationship in addition to being mother and son. I felt like her parent sometimes. I remember watching her deal with one of my younger brothers' death. He was thirteen months old when he died, and I saw my mother almost lose her mind. I stayed home from school with her while she was going through this. My older brother, my sister, and my father went back to their lives. My mother did not. I didn't go back to my life either. Everybody went through it, and I watched. I witnessed her going through that process in a way I don't think anybody else in my family did. I remember at one point making the conscious decision that because my mother had lost her baby, I was going to be a baby longer. I was probably about eight or nine, but I decided to still believe in Santa Claus. I made a willful decision to prolong my childhood so she would have a baby. And my mother in the middle of her grieving still had to function as a mother, as a teacher, as a wife. She still had to take care of business.

Mother was one of those women who kept on changing. She used to say that she was happiest in her life when she was in school. She would have loved to stay in school her entire life. She loved learning. She was in her fifties when she got her doctorate. My mother loved being around people, loved being around young people. She was exquisitely beautiful and delicate when she was young and became very handsome as she got older. Her skin had a certain kind of beauty to it; she never really wrinkled. My mother was very gentle, very smart, and she was capable of talking to anybody about anything. But what she was most passionate about were her children.

From the day I was born, I was obsessed with theater. I have absolutely no idea why. At school we would do these big end-of-the-year plays. Everybody would be in them. It was my favorite time of the year. I found so many outlets for who I was later to become. When my mother went to New York City to do some advanced degree work at New York University, she took me to see my first Broadway play. *Hair* was playing at the time but she wouldn't let me see it. I was about thirteen. So she took me to the Broadway revival of *Hello, Dolly!* with Pearl Bailey. It was very exciting, seeing black people on stage. Then we saw a revival of *West Side Story* at Lincoln Center. I remember so specifically leaning forward in my seat, and something in my imagination was given permission to exist. It was just bursting inside me.

When the cast album of *Purlie Victorious* came out, I wanted it, I wanted it, I wanted it. I was about fourteen. It was nowhere to be found in Frankfort, Kentucky, where I grew up. We searched all over for it. One day my mother went to Louisville for a meeting. When she came back, she called to me from upstairs.

"George," she said. "I thought I told you to clean up your room."

"I did," I yelled back.

"Come up here right now," she said.

I ran up the steps wondering, what is she talking about? And there sitting on my bed was the album *Purlie Victorious*. I remember that moment so joyfully. She knew it was something that was dear to my heart, and

she surprised me with it. A gift. At that time, acquiring pieces of the theater was like acquiring pieces of myself. So my mother was giving me pieces of what I was going to become.

It's funny, my mother nurtured my passion but then was horrified when I decided to do it for a living. It was like she would feed all of these things to me and then wonder at the same time why I was eating them. My parents' middle-class "Negro logic" told them that I should not be doing this, not when I could be a doctor or lawyer or preacher. But loving me and seeing what I loved is why my parents supported me every step of the way. They later came to all of my shows.

It was ten years of struggle from the time I graduated from college to *The Colored Museum,* my first professional success. When my plays got into the realm of Broadway, like *Jelly's Last Jam,* it was on a large enough scale that my mother and father could brag to all their friends. *Colored Museum* was written up in *Newsweek* and *Time,* and the bigger the success, the more my parents could brag. They loved coming to New York to hang out and walk around. I'd meet up with them at a store somewhere, and my mother would be trying on dresses. I'd walk up, and the saleslady would say, "So this must be the playwright...." My father would be talking to the security guard and the bag-check person, saying, "His last play was ..."

I'd say, "Please, stop it," and I'd cringe with embarrassment. But I was really very proud that they were proud of me. Because ten years of struggle is long enough when you're going through it yourself, and it probably seems even longer when you're watching somebody that you care about go through it. My parents would hint around sometimes: "We were talking to your Aunt Mildred and she was saying that if you don't make it in theater, it's all right for you to move on to something else." They would never say it themselves, because the couple of times they tried, I went off: "I'm out here trying to survive and I deal with all these obstacles...." I would do one of my little famous speeches like that. So they learned how to say what they felt indirectly. But they were extraordinarily supportive.

My mother and father worked no matter what the circumstance. Their attitude was do what you do no matter what, just go, do it, do it, do it. Accomplish, succeed, move on. Accomplish, succeed, keep going, keep going, keep going. You're tired, too bad, do it. You're falling apart, too bad, do it. Do it. So much of this mind-set was the rule of the land growing up in a segregated town, of being a part of that "talented tenth" shit. There was an expectation that you will soar for the race. They drilled into your head that white people think you aren't capable or competent, so you must prove otherwise. At the school I attended, racial pride was reinforced. We were taught that a black man invented the traffic light, a black man did this, a black person did that. A Negro person did this, a Negro person did that. So I had no racial inferiority complex at all.

Growing up, both my mother and my grandmother protected me. We used to say that my grandmother was "colored" and my mother was "a Negro." My mother was raised to be a Negro girl, which is, polite, groomed, all of that. Whereas a colored girl will do whatever. My mother was the little darling of the community. She would play the organ in church on Sundays. She would do ballet at socials. She was the perfect little thing when she was growing up. My grandmother, on the other hand, was a colored woman. She was a force of nature. And nobody messed with my grandmother Miss Addie. That's Addie Parker Lindsay President — I love her full name. She was ferocious on principle, whereas my mother had to feel a sense of violation to become ferocious. There are these two stories in my family that I remember quite vividly. They show a striking difference between my mother and my grandmother.

A white insurance man came to my grandmother's house while she was ironing. He was inside, and my grandmother said, "Take off your hat." He went on talking and she said again, "Take off your hat," and he continued talking. And then she said, "You have a choice: you can either take off your hat or I can throw this iron and knock it off." That's my grandmother.

The other story involved a white insurance salesman and my mother. He came by the house and called my mother Anna, not Mrs. Wolfe, but Anna. That was violation beyond existence. Now this is the difference between these two women: My mother didn't threaten to throw the iron or anything like that.

She plotted for weeks. She found out what the insurance man's white wife's name was. So the next time when he came to the house and called her Anna, she said to him, "How's Juanita?" That was my mother's act of defiance. That was her way of getting back. My grandmother's back there hurling grenades and stuff while my mother is there planning strategy.

I lived in a fully-textured black world, a world in which there were many different women, all mothers to me of sorts, who were giving me all these truths to develop a sense of my own significance and a sense of my own responsibility. My grandmother nurtured the fierce uncompromising warrior in me; Miss Bokler, my first-grade teacher, nurtured the artist in me; my aunt Catherine had one of the most brilliant senses of humor. Then my mother was the unifying force who brought it altogether. My father added a global perspective and understanding.

I remember when my mother died, I went up to see her body, and I thought, who's that? For the first time I had some understanding of how extraordinary the concept of soul really is. Because that was not my mother. She wasn't moving, she wasn't talking, she wasn't doing anything, just gone. Where is that force? Does it evaporate? I don't think so. It continues. It just continues. She is with me right now, right here, making sure I don't tell too many family secrets. It's nothing deep. She is just here with me.

255

This project celebrates the things in life that we hold dear – our families, our friends, our communities. From the depths of my heart I thank my community of people who helped me realize this vision: My wife, Maria Perez-Brown, who first made me believe that this project could be done, and then encouraged me, worked with me, and loved me every step of the way – I couldn't have done it without you. My parents, Joseph and Constance Brown, my grandmother, Vivian Brown, my grandfather, Chauncey Bergen, and my brother, Richard Brown – you all inspire every day of my life, you are my core. My extended family – especially the Motts, the Caldwells, the Browns, the Bergens, the Ruffins, and the Perez, the Grajales, and the Davis families – I cherish our closeness and the support you have given me.

There are friends who extended themselves – from reading and critiquing every word to being a sounding board to making sure I had a place to stay in the cities I visited – more than I could have ever imagined. In this body of work, there is a piece of all of you: Lisa "Bulletproof Diva" Jones, Lea Sanders, Curtis Simmons, Robert Pini, Rusty O'Kelley, Father Martini Shaw, Alice Norris, Gladys Perez, and Michelle Suite.

Many friends and colleagues shared their ideas, time, and resources to lend their support, and I am grateful: Joan Harrell (BT), Shelly Shepard, Suzanne Malveaux (BT), John Kelley, Julie Bidwell, Miguel Herra, Lise Funderburg, Susan Wilcox, Michael Webb, Marie Nazon, Richard Caldwell, Michel Boodrou, Dave McGloin, Miriam Weintraub, Bill Fitzgerald, Kathy Minton, Adrienne Lopez, Nancy Goldman, Eric Latsky, Michelle Paige Paterson, Mark Alexander, Eugenia Harvey, Kumiki Gibson, Paula Silas, Perez Minton Productions, Stanley Nelson, Calle Crossly, Greg Coy, Rodney Stringfellow, and Alexis George.

There have been some strong influences that helped me develop as a journalist to pursue a

257

project of this nature: I would like to thank the members of the Public Affairs Television family for letting me know early on that you can do good work with integrity. I thank ABC producers Paul and Holly Fine for demonstrating that caring about people is the heart of good journalism. Thank you for your ongoing support. I thank the journalists at CBS News, the professors at Columbia Journalism School, the IYLI family, the Gardere family, Joan Roth, James Stolz, Dr. K.C. Morrison, and all of my friends from Syracuse University. You have been a tremendous support system.

I thank Little, Brown and Company, especially my editor, Amanda Murray, for sharing my vision and making it even stronger; my agent, Jessica Wainwright, for understanding the importance of this project from our first meeting; and my researchers, Russell Torres and Heather Dubin, for their hard work and dedication to the project. I hope you are as proud of the end result as I am.

I am grateful to Adger W. Cowans for his beautiful photographs and the experience, wisdom, and talent he brought to the project to make it richer. Adger would like to also thank Lea Sanders, Delores and Jim Little, Shari Rosenheck, and Virginia Hall for their support. We thank Vincent Tcholakian for his exquisite prints and Herman Jaffee Transcriptions for carefully reproducing every recorded word onto paper.

I deeply thank all of the mothers and sons who shared their stories. There were more than could possibly be included in the book, and I especially want to thank Dr. James Comer, Hawthorne Smith, Jackie Lee, Jack Azimov, Danny, Russell, and the Reverend Joseph Simmons, George Preston, and Rahima Lateef and her sons for their contribution.

Finally, I would like to recognize all of the women who, like my mother, inspired me to write this book. Some of them have passed on but live in the hearts of their loved ones. All of these women are of great strength and have touched the lives of many: Nancy Ruffin, Etta Bergen, Vivian Brown, Emma Bergen, Juana Grajales, Eva Davis, Catherine Caldwell, Ann Mott, Aida Bergen, Bernice Mays, Geraldine Keyes, Patricia Nixon, Geraldine Williams, Claudine Hunt, Eva Simms, Leona Brown, Nora Steel, Ann Walling, Joan Folley, Lillian Hendry, Rosie Mercer, Joan Keller, Kay Johnson, Roberta Schank, Katherine Wilcox, Susie Frost, Marie-Marthe Gardere, Joan Williams, Sylvia Friend, Elizabeth Bowers, Gwendolyn Morton, Eliza Johnson, and all of the women who have helped shape the life of a black man.

We are eternally grateful.